Explaining Why You Lost

Reasoning in Arbitration

INTERNATIONAL CHAMBER OF COMMERCE
The world business organization

Edited by
Antonio Crivellaro
Mélida N. Hodgson

Reasoning in Arbitration
Explaining why you lost

International Chamber of Commerce (ICC)
Publications Department
33-43 avenue du Président Wilson
75116 Paris
France

ICC Publication No. 810E
ISBN: 978-92-842-0561-5

Contents

Foreword

by Yves Derains

International arbitrators enjoy a considerable freedom in the conduct of the proceedings and in the decisions they make on the merits of the case. Subject to few exceptions, their decisions are final. Although absence of jurisdiction, lack of independence or impartiality, breach of due process, excess of power and violation of international public policy may lead to the setting aside of an award, it is rarely the case of wrong decisions on the merits. There are very few jurisdictions where a superficial assessment of the facts or a misinterpretation of the contract are grounds for setting aside an award. The same applies to an inaccurate application of the law, with the exceptions of some common law countries, such as England and the United States.

Yet, the arbitrators must explain their decisions. The rules of most arbitral institutions, such as article 32(2) of the ICC Rules of Arbitration, require that an award include reasons, although neither under the New York Convention nor under the UNCITRAL Model Law the failure to state reasons constitutes a ground for setting aside arbitral awards. Moreover, article 31(2) of the UNCITRAL Model Law permits the parties to agree that reasons shall not be given. As a result, many national laws inspired by the UNCITRAL Model Law offer the same possibility to the parties, as well as some laws designed independently such as the English 1996 Arbitration Act (Art. 52(4)) or Swiss Law (art. 189(2) LDIP).

However, with the exception of specialized arbitrations such as quality arbitration, where the main task of the arbitrators is to assess the quality of a product, the parties generally refrain to grant the arbitrators the power to render awards without reasons. They are right to do so. Judges do not like awards without reasons and show a certain reluctance to enforce them, even when the arbitrators were permitted not to give reasons. I will never forget the ironic remark of a French judge, more than 30 years ago, invited to order the enforcement in France an award rendered in the US according to the rules of a professional association which did not require that reasons support the awards. The award was three lines long and condemned a party to pay three million dollars. The judge looked at the award and said, with a smile: one million per line! The lack of motivation could not be a ground for refusing the enforcement but it was crystal clear that any weakness in the award or in the proceedings that had generated it would not be treated with much indulgence. Some may be astonished by this attitude, as the control by judges of the reasons given by the arbitrators is very limited. Indeed, the control of the reasons of an award may easily lead to the review of its merits and judges are not authorized to enter into such a review. This would be forgetting that without reasons in the award, the control of due process and in particular of the right to be heard often becomes an artificial exercise. For example, what is the practical purpose of discussing whether the arbitrators could admit a last minute submission by a party without breaching due process if it is impossible to know whether they took it into consideration in their decision?

But it would be wrong to assume that the parties are reluctant to permit the arbitrators to render unreasoned awards just because they are afraid of the judges' reaction. The drafting of awards play a significant role in the duration of arbitration proceedings, as illustrated by the fact that, although the time limit to render the award under the ICC Rules of Arbitration is six months from the signature of the terms of reference, the arbitrators are expected to submit their draft award for scrutiny to the International Court of Arbitration three months after the hearing or the post hearing brief. This shows that drafting a reasoned award is a time consuming operation. Since the parties, rightly or wrongly, usually complain about the duration of arbitration proceedings, there is no doubt that they have a real interest in knowing the reasons upon which the award is based. Otherwise, they would be satisfied with unreasoned awards which can be drafted very rapidly.

It is usually said that the losing party is more interested than the winning party in understanding the reasons for the outcome of the proceeding. It is probably true and it justifies the title of this Dossier "Explaining Why You Lost, Reasoning in Arbitration". This is based on the reaction of the parties and their counsel when they receive an award. Everybody starts by the last page since nobody is prepared to read two hundred pages before the final decision. On the successful side, once the decision is known, the immediate reaction is to open a bottle of champagne. Reading the reasons may be deferred for rainy days. To the contrary, on the unsuccessful side, all the energy will be put in trying to understand the reasons for the failure. But it is not the end of the story. After sometime, the winning party will come back to the reasons. When applicable, they will want to know why they did not get all they were claiming and, more generally, they will be interested in fully understanding the reasons for their victory and the losing party defeat in order to draw lessons for the future. This explains that, although there is almost no control of the arbitrator's reasons by courts, that arbitrators have a responsibility towards the parties and towards the arbitration community at large to provide comprehensive reasons for their awards. The publication of awards recently introduced by ICC makes that responsibility even greater.

This Dossier XVIII of the ICC Institute of World Business law contributes to the definition of the extent of that responsibility. It was the object of the discussions held during the 39th Annual Conference of the ICC Institute on 17 December 2019. The program was prepared by two experienced members of the Institute Council, Antonio Crivellaro and Mélida N. Hodgson, who were able, with the support of contributors with huge expertise in their respective fields, to cover the various aspects of this fascinating subject and to provide practitioners and scholars with several new paths for reflection.

Introduction

How Well Reasoned Must an Award Be to Satisfy Non-waivable Legitimacy Requirements?

by Antonio Crivellaro

1. INTRODUCTIVE PROPOSITIONS

I wish to offer the following propositions as a general frame for this Institute Dossier.

First, I never experienced a case of total absence of reasons in an award. Pursuant to most arbitration laws and institutional rules in force worldwide, the reasoning is now strictly required by mandatory norms and only a few legal orders allow the parties to dispense the arbitrators with the duty to give reasons, if the parties so agree at the outset of the proceedings. A further, obvious, exception is the "award by consent", in which the reasoning is replaced by the terms of the settlement agreement stipulated by the parties and endorsed by the tribunal.

Apart from these rare exceptions, we should therefore take for granted that the reasoning is a constant presence in all awards. Accordingly, the articles in this publication will not, presumably, wonder whether the reasons must be part of an award, but rather discuss what adequacy standard the reasons should meet. In other words, we will assume that "failure of reasons" is tantamount to "failure of adequate reasons" to then embark on the search for the minimum threshold to meet the adequacy or sufficiency standard in the reasoning that speakers and participants consider necessary.

Second, arbitral reasoning should be viewed distinctly from judicial reasoning. A badly or wrongly reasoned judgment remains subject to appeal and will be reviewed on both facts and law. It is because of this circumstance that the quality of the Court's reasoning may be relatively lower without causing irreparable harm to the parties. However, the appeal is not a remedy available to review or rectify an award, which remains "final" although potentially unsatisfactory or deficient on facts or law. It is this essential distinction that makes the arbitrators' task, when drafting the reasoning, significantly more burdensome and sensitive than the equivalent task of a State lower Court.[1]

The difference is no surprise for the following reason. The Court is a State organ committed to render justice in accordance with the State legal order. It is obviously accountable to the public for improprieties or wrongdoings in administering justice, but not bound by any duty towards the parties in the individual case to frame the reasons of the judgment according to defined quality standards. The arbitrator is instead a "private judge" owning to the parties a duty to fulfil the mandate with diligence and care, which includes the duty to provide reasons understandable to the parties, by which he/she is remunerated. His/her principal duty is to render a decision that, in conformity with the parties' expectations, shall be exhaustively responsive to their claims, arguments and defenses.

In simpler terms, the arbitrator's task is greater, but so is his/her paycheck.

Third, for what concerns the legal reasoning, arbitrators should be reminded that the principle *jura novit curia* is of limited application in international arbitration. Whereas the factual reasoning requires no more than a careful analysis of the evidence in the record, the legal reasoning may face a cultural difficulty which is a typical feature of arbitration. By common experience, the members of a tribunal may be educated in a legal order different from the applicable law chosen by the parties so that the latter will be viewed as a "foreign" law from the arbitrators' perspective. This peculiarity is currently much less troubling than when I was young. At that time, application of foreign law fluctuated between two alternative approaches, both drawn from State court proceedings: either the foreign law was treated as a question of fact (common law jurisdictions) left essentially to the parties' burden of proof; or was treated as a question of law (civil law jurisdictions), left to the autonomous determination of the arbitrators under the adagio *juria novit curia* enabling them to apply whatever law *ex officio* and even irrespective of the parties' submissions in law.

However, neither one proved suitable in international arbitration. Being a creature of the parties' consent, the arbitral process may be shaped more flexibly than the process before courts and, over the years, a better-balanced approach was specifically tailored for arbitration. This consists of a constructive cooperation and dialogue between parties and tribunals to correctly ascertain the contents of the applicable law: the parties provide the tribunal with the sources of law and their reading of the legal texts supported by case-law; the tribunals are not confined to the information received from the parties and have the power to *sua sponte* inquire about the contents of the law they must apply, however with an important limitation that directly affects their legal reasoning.

The limitation consists in the following. When autonomously interpreting the law they have to apply, before framing their reasoning by adopting a legal interpretation which was never raised nor pleaded by the parties, the arbitrators must give them a reasonable opportunity to be heard. By failing to so do, the tribunal will take the parties by surprise in the final award and this would be tantamount to a breach of due process and lead to annulment of the award, particularly when the arbitrators' *ex officio* construction of the law proves to be decisive for the outcome of the case.

In my view, this is one of the most crucial issues when drafting the reasoning section of an award: it indeed requires particular caution by the arbitrators, who should timely (i.e. before final deliberation) consult the parties on the legal issue concerned, to avoid finding themselves too late to do so in light of the time-limit to render the award.

Fourth, another mantra is the "sufficiency" or "adequacy" of the reasoning as an inseparable component of the duty to give reasons. Does this mean "exhaustiveness" implying that the award should address not only all questions, but also all allegations, arguments or defences raised by the parties? It is common practice for the parties to support a claim or a defence or objection on multiple alternative or sometimes cumulative arguments. Does a well-reasoned award need to take a position on every and all such arguments?

In investment disputes, Article 48(3) of the ICSID Convention provides that "*The award shall deal with* **every question** *submitted to the Tribunal, and shall state the reasons upon which it is based*". Article 47(1)(j) specifies that one of the essential elements that must appear in the award is "t*he decision of the Tribunal on every question submitted to it together with the reasons upon which the decision is based*". According to legal literature, a similar approach is shared in international commercial arbitration

However, the "every question" requirement is to be construed reasonably. As case-law and legal literature show, a distinction should be maintained between "question", on the one hand, and "argument" or "allegation" or "plea", on the other hand. The "question" is the issue that has a bearing on the resolution of the case and cannot be left undecided, otherwise giving rise to an *infra petitum* which in most legislations is a ground for annulment.[2] In order to resolve the specific "question", a tribunal must of course consider all arguments and counter-arguments, but is not bound to decide them all where it finds that some of the arguments are prevailing or absorb the others.[3]

The only admissible exception is the case in which two "questions" are apparently distinct but in realty strictly intertwined. In such a case, a prudent tribunal does not omit to consider both "questions" but may validly rule, providing the relevant reasons, that "question A" is related to, or encompasses, "question B" and the decision on "B" is absorbed by the decision on "A". This would be a perfectly adequate reasoning, allowing readers to understand that both "questions" were duly considered and that the necessary reasoning is not missing. This was the approach recommended by the International Court of Justice and adopted by ICSID ad hoc Committees in annulment proceedings.[4]

Fifth, the reasoning is required since it provides the only tool allowing for control over the legitimacy of the arbitral process: was due process respected? Were the parties provided with a reasonable opportunity to be heard? Did the tribunal decide by applying the law it was mandated to apply? And so on: I will provide below a longer checklist of all the "musts" that a reasoning should satisfy for various purposes, however it appears evident that procedural legitimacy cannot be checked when reasons are so vague as to leave unanswered the above questions. In similar cases, the reasoning is missing because no controller may infer whether the award withstands the legitimacy test or is, on the contrary, the product or arbitrariness.[5]

Sixth (and last), several chapters will make the case that the purpose of a good reasoning is to make the award "convincing" to the readers, and even "persuasive" to the losing party. This is correct, but we should recall that two-thousand-four-hundred years ago Aristotle had already come to the same conclusion. In his view, rhetoric is the typical "*art of persuasion*" or the "*ability of observing in any given case the available means of persuasion*", an art implemented in three modes: *ethos*, that is the "*power of evincing a personal character which makes oneself credible*"; *pathos*, that is the "*power of stirring the emotions of the recipients*"; and *logos*, that is the "*power of proving the truth, or an apparent truth, by means of persuasive arguments*".[6]

Approximately three centuries after Aristotle, Cicero underlined in his monumental work *De Oratore*, also known as *De Eloquentia*, that advocacy was typically an intellectual art to persuade the audience through *elocutio* or *loquendi elegantia*.[7]

Therefore, we are not "reinventing the wheel" so to speak. Legal techniques have progressed (or perhaps regressed?), but legal reasoning has maintained the fascinating components of a rhetorical mission exactly as depicted centuries ago by Aristotle and Cicero.[8]

2. THE CHECKLIST FOR ESTABLISHING WHETHER THE AWARD IS WELL-REASONED

I strongly hope that a consensus will be reached to qualify an award as adequately reasoned *if* it meets the prerequisites enumerated in the following checklist.

An award is not satisfactorily reasoned in one or more of the following cases:

i. The reader, especially the Court which is approached for either enforcing or annulling the award, is unable to understand the logical itinerary (the *ratio decidendi*) followed by the tribunal, i.e., is unable to understand how the tribunal has proceeded from one point to the other and eventually to its conclusions.[9]

ii. The award fails to identify at the outset the issues to be decided.

iii. The award does not allow one to infer whether the tribunal has duly considered both parties' positions on points of fact or of law, including the determination of the applicable law when this is a disputed issue.

iv. The award does not permit one to ascertain whether the tribunal has taken into consideration only the evidence provided by the parties, as it should, or whether it was influenced by pieces of information known to the arbitrators but unknown to the parties, or never pleaded during the proceedings, or whether it simply failed to consider and assess the evidence provided by the parties.[10]

v. The award does not allow one to understand whether the tribunal has applied the agreed governing law, or what law it has applied, if any.

vi. The award does not allow one to understand whether the tribunal has exceeded its mission by omitting a relevant issue (*infra petita*), or deciding an issue which was not referred by the parties to the tribunal (*extra petita*), in short whether the final decision exactly mirrors the claims and/or counterclaims as lodged by the parties.

vii. The award does not clarify whether the contractual provisions from which the dispute arises, and the parties have discussed before the tribunal treating them as relevant to the issues in dispute, have been taken into account or applied.

viii. The award simply mentions the contract clauses that the tribunal has read but fails to address the tribunal's findings concerning their interpretation, or the reasons for those findings.

ix. The reasoning does not show internal consistency and does not appear congruent with deliberation process recorded in the award.[11]

x. The award leaves unclear whether the claims or objections submitted by the parties have been understood or misunderstood.

xi. Even more importantly, the award leaves unclear whether the decision is influenced by a legal or contractual interpretation internally debated within the tribunal *ex officio* at the deliberation stage, however never pleaded by the parties before the tribunal, thus breaching the principle of *contradictoire*.

3. SOME CONCLUSIVE REMARKS

To close my introduction, I offer to readers the following preliminary conclusions.

3.1 In the search for an adequacy standard

I take the liberty to share what I consider to be the best definition of adequate reasoning. One was given by the *Soufraki Ad Hoc* Committee when requested to annul a previous award under Article 52 (1) of the ICSID Convention. According to this annulment committee, the expression of reasons is in substance

> the only way by which compliance with the fundamental prohibition of manifest excess of powers and with the critical duty to apply the proper law may be observed... the more lucid and explicit the reasons set out by a Tribunal, the easier it should be to observe what a Tribunal is in fact doing by way of compliance.[12]

The second was given by another ICSID *Ad Hoc* Committee in *M.I.N.E.*, according to which, "*as long as the award enables the reader to follow how the Tribunal proceeded from point A. to point B. and eventually to its conclusions*", the requirement to state reasons is at least satisfied at its minimum level and the award stands.[13]

Thus, a reasoning which has evident *lacunae* on important points of fact or law, prevents one from understanding the Tribunal's *ratio decidendi*. The *lacuna* makes it impossible to understand how the Tribunal arrived at certain conclusions instead of others. It particularly prevents checking whether the Tribunal has applied the law that it had to apply, or whether it was inspired by self-made considerations, manifestly exceeding its mission. In such conditions, the award cannot stand.

3.2 Avoiding arbitrariness

A reasoning which is laconic in some parts and opaque or puzzling in others, does not guarantee that the award is based on objective and rational grounds. On the contrary, it sheds doubts on the possibility that the Tribunal's findings be arbitrary on points of fact or of law, including the determination of the applicable law. This is why providing express reasons is the only means to test the arbitrators' compliance with the fundamental duty not to exceed their powers and to safeguard due process, as lucidly stated in the Soufraki decision on annulment.

Personally, I would never advise a party to accept renouncing to the reasoning, which is tantamount to empowering an arbitral tribunal to adjudicate "as it deems fit". Too many risks are run when taking a similar approach, first and foremost, the absolute arbitrariness of the decision in plain disregard of the parties' positions as argued before the Tribunal.

3.3 The educative function of the reasoning—contribution to improving the law

At a time when the arbitration community was still discussing whether to favor reasoned awards or unreasoned awards, Professor Carbonneau stated, quite rightly in my view, that reasoning in the awards contributes to form "*a better basis for the elaboration of a common law of international transactions than national court decisions*".[14]

Justice Bingham and Toby Landau share the above opinion and add a further benefit potentially provided by a good and credible reasoning. They, in particular, agree that the giving of reasons may provide an essential guide not only to the disputing parties in the individual case, but also to all other interested parties involved in future similar disputes to allow them to "*learn from the forensic experience of others*".[15]

I find this view attractive: qualifying the reasoning as a guide for future conduct is, at the same time, a lesson to the arbitrators soliciting their utmost care in drafting the reasons, and a lesson imparted to arbitration practitioners in comparable situations. In investment arbitrations, this is the regular case: as we know, awards in investment disputes are frequently crafted in a didactic way to progressively create uniform international investment law, but also some important commercial arbitral awards are quoted as "leading" or "guiding" decisions in subsequent awards or in doctrinal comments.

NOTES

1. See Lord Justice Bingham, "Reasons and Reasons for Reasons: Differences between a Court Judgment and an Arbitration Award", in *Arbitration International*, 1997, pp. 141 ff.
2. See the decision of the Swiss Federal Tribunal dated 16 May 2011 in *DG Engineering GmbH v Inotis Sàrl*. The Federal Tribunal annulled an arbitral award on the ground that the tribunal had omitted to deal with and decide an issue raised by one party, which was relevant to the disposal of the dispute and, if considered, might have reversed the outcome of the case. The annulment was based on the breach of the "right to be heard" in the meaning of Article 190(2)(d) of the Swiss Private International Law. The decision is published in ASA Bulletin, September 2011, with an interesting comment by François Perret, *Quelques considérations à propos de la motivation des sentences arbitrales en matière d'arbitrage international à la lumière d'une jurisprudence récente du Tribunal Fédéral*. Professor Perret quite rightly observed that the most serious defect in the annulled award was the insufficient reasoning, a defect that may lead to annulment of the award when it becomes apparent that the tribunal has left untouched a question on which the tribunal had been requested to take determination.
3. On the adequacy of reasoning in investment and commercial arbitrations, see P. Lalive, "On the Reasoning of International Arbitral Awards", in *Journal of International Dispute Settlement*, 2010, pp. 55-65. For the suggestion that the reasoning should not be excessively lengthy but focused on the essential points that lead to the decision, see R. Dupeyré, "Les limites de l'obligation de motivation: de la concision des sentences arbitrales", in *Revue Qubécoise du Droit International*, 2006, pp. 44-51.
4. See the ICJ Advisory Opinion dated 12 July 1973 in the case *Application for Review of Judgment No. 158 of The United Nations Administrative Tribunal*, 1973 ICJ Reports, pp. 210/211. This was also the approach followed in the Decision on Annulment of the *ad hoc* Committee in *Lucchetti v Peru*, § 127 and in ICSID Case No. ARB/81/2, *Klöckner Industrie-Anlagen GmbH and Others v Republic of Cameroon*, Decision on Annulment, 3 May 1985. For a case-law analysis in investment and commercial arbitration, see A. Crivellaro, The Failure to State Reasons in ICSID

Awards, in The Paris Journal of International Arbitration, 2012-4, pp. 865-881; A. Crivellaro, Annulment of ICSID Awards: Back to the "First Generation"?, in Liber Amicorum en l'honneur de Serge Lazareff, Pedone, Paris, June 2011, pp. 145-175.

5. According to T. Landau, the requirement that the award be adequately reasoned constitutes a "*safeguard against arbitrariness or biased judgment, or private judgment, or irrational splitting of the differences between the parties*" and is the "*litigants' guarantee that [..] justice should not only be done, but should manifestly and undoubtedly be seen to be done*": see T. Landau, "Reasons for Reasons: the Tribunal's Duty in Investor-State Arbitration, Report at ICCA Conference 2008", in *ICCA Congress Series*, Volume 14, Kluwer Law International, 2009, pp. 187-205.

6. A Crivellaro, "An Art, a Science or a Technique?", in *Arbitration Advocacy in Changing Times*, ICCA Congress Series, Volume 15 (ICCA 2010 Congress in Rio de Janeiro), Kluwer Law International, 2011, pp. 9-24.

7. Ibid., p. 9.

8. On the need for the reasons provided in international awards to be persuasive, see *inter alia* Justice Lord Humphrey LLoyd, "Writing Awards, a Common Lawyer's Perspective", in *ICC International Arbitration Bulletin*, Vol. V, No. 1, 1994, pp. 38-45.

9. For a comparative analysis of domestic Courts' approach when reviewing arbitral awards, see T. H. Webster, "Review of Substantive Reasoning in International Arbitral Awards by National Courts: Ensuring One-Stop Adjudication", in *Arbitration International*, Vol. 22, No. 3, LCIA, 2006; F. Madsen and P. Eriksson, "Deliberations of the Arbitral Tribunal - Analysis of Reasoned Awards from Swedish Perspective", in *Stockholm International Arbitration Review*, 2006, pp. 1-42, at p. 17 ff.

10. Failure to refer to evidence in the file may be a decisive omission leading to annulment. On 8 January 2018, the Tribunal Superior de Justicia de Madrid set aside an award dated 6 April 2017 for "*lack of motivation*" on the ground that the arbitrator made no reference to the evidence he had relied on to establish the dispositive section of the award: see R. Irra, F. Fortùn and C. Cachat, "The Obligation to Motivate an Award: An Open Door to the Substantive Review of an Award?", in *ICC Dispute Resolution Bulletin*, 2018, Issue 4, *Global Developments*, pp. 27 ff.

11. A. S. Rau, "On Integrity in Private Judging", in *Arbitration International*, Vol. 14, No. 2, 1998, pp. 115-156.

12. ICSID Case No. ARB/02/7, *Hussein Nuaman Soufraki v United Arab Emirates*, Decision on the Application for Annulment, 5 June, 2007, § 127.

13. ICSID Case No. ARB/84/4, *M.I.N.E. v Republic of Guinea*, Decision on Annulment, 22 December, 1989, § 5.09.

14. T. E. Carbonneau, "Rendering Arbitral Awards with Reasons: the Elaboration of Common Law of International Transactions", in *23 Columbia Journal Transnational Law*, 1985, pp. 578-614, at p. 597.

15. T. Landau, cit. *supra*, footnote 5, p. 188, quoting from Lord Bingham.

Chapter 1
Reasoning in Arbitration

by Charles Jarrosson*

I. INTRODUCTION

Everyone knows that there can be no trial nor court decision worthy of those names without due process as this principle is the very essence of a trial. But this does not apply to the reasoning of court decisions, which is not consubstantial to the proceedings. One has always stated that Divine justice need not be reasoned: indeed, the Lord need not explain, for His decision is necessarily right and fair. Those who speak in His name are not required to explain.

Human justice, for its part, must rely on reason, on the law, and cannot be subject to arbitrariness. Setting out the tribunal's reasoning is, by far, the preferred way of showing that the solution was not arbitrary and that justice has been rendered: indeed, "Justice must not only be done, it must also be seen to be done."[1]

However, it is only very recently that the practice of setting out reasons for court decisions has become widely accepted. Indeed, for a long time, it was usual practice that the judge simply offered a solution without explaining it. Thus, history teaches that setting out reasons for court decisions is relatively recent. Accursius, famous erudite of the Middle Ages (glossator), had even considered that court decisions should not in principle provide reasons.[2] In France, the duty to state reasons was imposed during the Revolution (laws of 16-24 August 1790), but it had appeared two centuries earlier in Florence or in Spain, in the province of Aragon.[3] In England, as noted by J.-L. Delvolvé, given the characteristics of the procedure and the work done by the parties in terms of fact-finding and evidence, the duty to state reasons is not as entrenched in legal tradition as it is in romano-germanic legal systems.[4]

Turning now to arbitration, whether to set out the legal reasoning of awards may appear to be one of those well-settled questions that do not raise any particular issue. An author even considered that, in recent years, rare were the subject matters that have raised as little interest as the reasoning of awards![5] Indeed, there is a certain unanimity in this regard, which can be easily explained: the basic principle is that awards should be set out their reasons. This reflects what most texts require, what parties or arbitration institutions wish for and what arbitrators do in practice. But if one takes a closer look and analyses the last few decades, one realises that things have, somewhat, evolved.

In order to encompass this evolution and assess the present situation, we can ask a few simple questions:

* Professor of Law, University of Paris II (Panthéon-Assas), France; Editor, *Revue de l'arbitrage*

- Should an arbitrator state his reasons? (see section II below);
- What does setting out reasoning actually mean? (see section III);
- Why should an arbitrator state his reasons? (see section IV); and
- What is the appropriate standard of review in respect of the reasons stated in arbitral decisions? (see section V).

II. SHOULD AN ARBITRATOR STATE HIS REASONS?

The decision-maker is not always keen to disclose the reasons underpinning his decision. Indeed, being compelled to give reasons entails the risk of being exposed to criticism and, thereby, losing a bit of one's authority. It is in this light that we should understand Lord Mansfield's well-known advice to his fellow judges in the 18th century: "Consider what you consider justice requires and decide accordingly. But never give your reasons; for your judgment will probably be right, but your reasons will certainly be wrong."[6] What is amusing is that, at that very moment, in France, Daniel Jousse, an 18th century prominent French lawyer, was saying exactly the same thing, and Talleyrand will not write anything different in his *Mémoires*[7] one century later.

However, international laws and conventions now practically always include an obligation to give reasons (although French arbitration law does not require it).[8] This obligation is sometimes expressly provided for (see e.g., Belgian Judicial Code (art. 1713(4°), Italian Code of civil procedure, (art. 823-5 CCP). It is also the case under French domestic law (art. 1482(2) CCP). But, under French law, in international cases, the provisions regarding the content of arbitral awards would seem to require reasons to be given in the award. However, as we shall see later, the issue is not as clear-cut as it would seem. The Washington Convention does impose the obligation to reason the decision.[9]

It is often the case that the parties are free to waive this obligation: in this sense, there is only a presumption that the award should include its reasons. This is the solution adopted by English Law, under the 1979 Arbitration Act, and later under the 1996 Arbitration Act (Art. 52(4)), by Swiss Law (art. 189(2) LDIP), just like the UNCITRAL Model Law (art. 31.2) or the Geneva Convention (art. VII).

One should stress that, although certain laws authorise the parties to relieve the arbitrators from having to state their reasons in their awards, in practice, they very seldom do. One would be hard put to find what would be the incentive for the parties not knowing the reasoning behind the solution imposed on them by an award, especially if this has no impact on the arbitrators' fees.

Arbitration has been impacted by the way ideas have evolved with regard to due process. The right to a fair trial, as developed over time by the European Court of Human Rights, also implies the duty to state reasons. The latter has a somewhat special place because it is considered to be part and parcel of the fundamental right to a fair trial while, at the same time, being open to adjustments. Indeed, the European Court of Human Rights admits that the obligation to give reasons may vary depending on the nature of the decision and considers that it should be examined in light of all the circumstances of the case.

In short, the rule is easy to formulate: unless the parties decide otherwise (when such a decision is necessary), the rule is the obligation for the arbitrators to state reasons in their awards. Therefore, the interesting question is not whether arbitrators should articulate reasons in their award but, rather, what providing reasons actually means and then why provide reasons at all and, finally, how to review the reasons provided in the award.

III. WHAT DOES STATING REASONS ACTUALLY MEAN?

It might be useful to define what is meant by "stating the reasons" or the "motivation" for an award. In latin languages, the etymology is interesting: it comes from *motus*: movement, and *movere*: to move. *Motivation* or *motivazione* or *motivación* (which means "justification" in French or Italian or Spanish) is what encourages you to go in that direction, it is the expression of what leads your opinion in this direction rather than any other. Thus, reasoning is a rational approach of the mind. But reasoning, when we are judging, is not merely an internal approach because it requires that our thought process to find a solution to the question raised be externalised with the help of words.

This attempt at defining what "providing reasons" means already enables us to see what it is not: for instance, when an arbitrator sums up a party's position and then writes: "the tribunal shares this opinion", there is no legal reasoning, it is simply sloth. Efficient arbitration institutions do notice this and share their observations with arbitrators so that they have to explain why they chose to uphold the arguments of one party, which usually also requires them to explain why they rejected the other party's arguments. A review of arbitral awards shows that they are becoming longer and longer, even though this is not always due to the section relating to the "reasoning" but, rather, to the section which "sums up the positions of the parties". Be that as it may, on the one hand, the growing demands of the arbitration institutions and, on the other, the tendency to draft awards in such a manner that simply reading them will allow for a full understanding of the case have played a role in encouraging this trend.

There are different types of arbitrations or awards; are there also different types of reasoning or specific reasoning? This question should be answered in the affirmative and it is precisely in this regard that this matter has evolved.

Is there any point in giving reasons in an **award by consent**? One might wonder since, in this type of award, the parties themselves have found the solution. Explaining their own solution to them is useless: the rationale for stating reasons has disappeared. In concrete terms, an arbitrator who accepts to render an award which embodies the agreement of the parties need not give further reasons than a standard formulation which could read: "The parties have agreed to this or that solution; it does not, in my opinion, violate Public Policy and, therefore, I echo these elements as mine". This is why the 1986 Dutch Law, and also the UNCITRAL Model Law (art. 31.2), have expressly chosen to waive this requirement in relation to consent awards.

Awards rendered in **trade associations arbitration** cases (such as commodity trading and shipping) are worth analysing. Reading though one such award, one may have the impression that there is no legal reasoning. In fact, the reasoning exists, but it is extremely simplified given the specific nature of the dispute which relates to the quality of the goods. In this context, arbitrators are in essence technicians who can confine themselves to testing a set of requirements and drawing the necessary inferences. As Lord Bingham wrote: "There are some arbitrations, those of the 'look-sniff' variety in particular, where there is really no room for the giving of reasons: tapioca pellets either are, in the experienced judgment of a trade arbitrator, of fair average quality or they are not; whichever way his opinion goes there is probably not much that he can usefully add by way of exegesis."[10]

Does *ex æquo et bono* arbitration or **amiable composition** change anything? It does not, as far as the obligation to give reasons is concerned, but admittedly it influences the style of the reasoning. Indeed, the arbitrator no longer bases his reasoning solely on the applicable rules of law but must also explain the reasons why he or she chooses to depart from them, as the case may be. He must clearly set out the reasons why the outcome of the cause would be inequitable had he confined himself to applying the legal rules or give his reasons to hold that the legal solution appears equitable on the facts. In practice, the reasoning will tend to focus much more on all the circumstances of the case.

This publication devotes a chapter to the distinction between **commercial arbitration and investment arbitration**. In principle, the obligation to state reasons applies equally to both fields. But as regards the reasoning itself, one might perceive some differences, because, amongst other things, investment arbitration usually places a greater reliance on precedents, i.e. past awards addressing similar issues.

However, a careful review of awards shows that, whatever the type of award, certain set phrases and practices are routinely resorted to by arbitrators in order to avoid subsequent challenges. Such precautions often relate to the procedure applied by the arbitrators or their general approach. In this regard, I am not of the opinion that there should be a fundamental distinction in the legal reasoning expected of arbitrators depending on whether their background is one of civil law or common law.

There is another question which is beginning to stir up controversy and that I shall only mention: there is a growing trend in favour of publishing arbitral awards coupled with the development of artificial intelligence. Will this not lead to changes in the way arbitrators set out their reasoning, possibly towards a more frequent use of standard and formulaic reasons?

We have just seen that giving reasons for an award does not always mean the same thing depending on the type of award or the context. This far, however, a question has remained in the shadows and we need to tackle it: why should one give reasons for the decision?

IV. WHY SHOULD AN ARBITRATOR STATE HIS REASONS?

The question is: *why should one give reasons?* The answer lies in the answer to another question, i.e. whom are the reasons intended for? There are as many answers to this question as there are recipients. Indeed, the legal reasoning offered in support of a decision fulfils different functions that are common to both civil law and common law despite their different legal traditions.

In this matter, a distinction should be made depending on the parties, the arbitration institutions involved and, later, the court that might be asked to review the award. But one should also not forget the arbitrator himself and that is where I suggest we start.

The arbitrator Indeed, we tend to forget one of the main functions of giving reasons, if not its central purpose, because it comes before the award itself and relates to its drafting. Fleshing out the reasons in writing helps the person who decides: it compels the decision-maker to formulate logically the thought process which has led him from the evidence and legal arguments of the parties to his solution. Jules Renard, who was well known for his wit, used to say: "Once I have decided, I hesitate for a long time." It is a joke, but not only a joke. As a matter of fact, we, arbitrators, very often have an idea of what the outcome should be, even before settling for a particular reasoning. Legal reasoning moves backwards: from the intuitive solution to the facts. Articulating legal reasons for a particular outcome enables arbitrators to check the soundness of the assumption. Facing seemingly insuperable difficulties in the drafting sometimes serves as a cue that the solution is not robust enough, or even mistaken and should be dropped.

The parties The main function the reasons stated in the award serve is to justify and explain the chosen solution to the parties and, first and foremost, to the losing party who wishes to know why this is the case, why his arguments or pieces of evidence failed to win over the tribunal. The winning party is more interested in the last page of the award and will soon forget being disappointed with the reasons for the award as long as the eventual award is favourable to him.

The reasons given in awards are more detailed than in court decisions. This is due to the fact that disputes often involve significant amounts and are complex, but also to the fact that, arbitrators being remunerated, parties expect them to make a conscious effort to show that they have considered every argument. Moreover, offering a thorough legal reasoning is certainly a pedagogic endeavour on the part of arbitrators. This is important and characteristic of arbitration because the end game is not only to render a valid award but to go beyond and guarantee its *acceptability*[11] by making it convincing.

The way reasons are set out in awards varies according to the arbitrator: they each have their own style, depending on the case or mode of thinking, each one may wish to emphasise legal arguments, factual elements or evidence, etc.

There are differences between awards and court decisions in terms of the purposes the reasons serve. Obviously, in both cases reasoning is a rampart against arbitrary decisions, but a court decision must be reasoned for reasons of its own that do not exist in arbitration, at least in commercial arbitration. Justice is public and stating reasons is one aspect of its democratic character. Arguably, as investment arbitration cases often touch on issues of public policy, there is a strong case for making awards in this field available to the public.

Individual opinions, when dissenting, raise specific problems. Indeed, as a matter of principle, dissenting opinions are not part of the award; they cannot, therefore, be considered part of the reasons for the award; moveover, even if they were to state reasons for anything, it would relate mainly to a solution which is the opposite of the solution ultimately upheld. Separate opinions, i.e. concurring opinions based on different grounds, seem to have a different status because they also justify the chosen solution, even though for reasons that differ from the majority award: they just form part of the award.

The arbitration institution Some rules—and the ICC rules feature prominently in this regard—provide that the draft award be submitted to the institution for a formal review. The scrutiny of ICC is very extensive and mainly relates to the legal reasoning. In so doing, ICC acts in the interest of the parties who will receive the award and in contemplation of a potential judicial review of the award. The objective is, therefore, twofold: make sure that the award is intelligible for the parties and that there are no irregularities affecting the validity of the award. The arbitral tribunal's legal reasoning may be challenged for being deficient, insufficient, unrelated to the arguments raised, or inconsistent. There is obviously a fine line between objecting to deficient reasoning and disagreeing with the findings the tribunal made on the merits. It should be noted that in practice, arbitral institutions when scrutinising the quality of the reasoning in awards, tend not to take into account the applicable law as chosen by the parties, nor the law of the place of arbitration, but rather, insist on thorough reasoning, even on matters such as the quantification of the damages. While French law, for instance, does not require detailed explanations and considers that the determination of the amount of damages should be left to the discretion of the court or the arbitral tribunal, and while the *Cour de cassation* itself ruled that the judge is under no obligation to specify the factors that contributed to the assessment,[12] conversely, ICC takes the opposite view and, even in relation to awards rendered in France, upholds a similar rule to that which exists in English law since the 1966 *Ward v James* case.[13]

The judge with powers of judicial review The reasons stated in the award is of particular interest for the judge who will review the award, either within the framework of setting aside proceedings or that of enforcement proceedings of a foreign award. Stating reasons for the decision is, as we saw, a guarantee of a proper administration of justice for it allows for an efficient review of the decision and clarifies its scope. Indeed, the scope of *res judicata* often depends on the interpretation of the reasons which are, if one believes in the maxim *Res judicata pro veritate habetur*, an expression of the truth.

But, as far as the judge is concerned, the crux of the matter is to determine *whether* the reasoning can be subject to review and if so, what the standard of review should be. We will therefore end this whistle-stop tour with the applicable standard of review.

V. WHAT IS THE APPROPRIATE STANDARD OF REVIEW IN RELATION TO THE DUTY TO STATE REASONS?

Who reviews and how? Chronologically, it can be the arbitration institution and, more frequently, the court when dealing with setting aside proceedings or the enforcement of foreign awards. The role of arbitration institutions has already been depicted, all that remains to be addressed now is the review carried out by the court. I will, intentionally, deal only briefly with this important point because it would take a whole day to deal with it thoroughly.

At the outset, an important distinction to be drawn concerns the scope of the review: either a *substantive* review of the award on the *merits* or a more *formal* review comes to mind. The dividing line between the two is very blurred. In this regard, determining whether reasons are stated in the award is a special case: does this involve a review of the merits or simply a formal assessment taking the award at face value? If it suffices to confirm that reasons, whatever they may be, are in fact stated, it is obviously formal. However, to the extent that the essence of the reasons themselves—whether they are adequate and consistent—is challenged, it is a question of merits. Let us now take these two types of review one by one.

The review of the *existence* of reasoning, considered as a formal review, is assessed according to the applicable law which, as we saw earlier, often requires that reasons be given, but which could accept certain nuances or exceptions if it is provided for in the law or if the parties so wish. Total failure to state reasons is rare and the setting aside of awards on those grounds is just as rare.

It is worth noting that neither under the New York Convention nor under the UNCITRAL Model Law the failure to state reasons constitutes a ground for setting aside arbitral awards. Those jurisdictions, which require awards to state their reasons, do not necessarily consider that it would be against international public policy to enforce, in their country, an award rendered under a law that accepts to waive this obligation. The French Cour de Cassation has consistently taken this approach in its jurisprudence since the Elmassian case[14] in 1960, and this rule has now found its way into art. 1483 of the Code of Civil Procedure according to which the failure to state reasons only constitutes a ground for annulment in relation to domestic arbitral awards. However, it is important to note a very recent decision by the Paris Court of Appeal dated 2 April 2019 which took the opposite view; holding that the obligation for

> judicial decisions to state their reasons is an element of the right to a fair trial. Arbitrators who fail to state reasons for their decisions disregard the scope of their mission and recognition of an award devoid of legal reasons goes against the French conception of International Public Policy.[15]

It is too early to say whether this corresponds to a reversal of jurisprudence, all the more so since a June 2019 decision seems to revert to the traditional solution.[16]

Assessing the *relevance* of reasoning, in fact, is akin to revising the award: this review is generally excluded. Reviewing the quality of the reasoning is a delicate task. To put this issue into perspective, let us examine two different legal systems: the French and the English.

The French case law has undergone interesting changes in relation to conflicting reasons. Originally contradictory reasons in arbitral awards and court decisions alike were thought to cancel each other out so to speak: thus, the award was not deemed to be reasoned. French law later evolved and opted for the opposite solution but only in respect of arbitral awards. From now on, it is not only irrelevant whether the reasons provided were apposite to the case at hand but also, as we just saw, whether the law was correctly applied or whether the legal reasoning evinces potential contradictions. Under French law, it therefore suffices that reasons—whether or not legally correct—are stated in the award.[17]

More often than not, review of the merits is excluded, at least in most cases. However, some legal systems may, without allowing for a review of the merits, offer the possibility of striking down awards where the reasoning reveals a major legal mistake. English law is interesting in this particular regard: appeals on points of law (art. 69 Arb. Act) exist, but it is possible to waive this right, most notably by selecting arbitration rules in their arbitration agreement that exclude any right to appeal the award. In the USA, review of the manifest disregard of the law has become less frequent since the 25 March 2008 *Hall Street v Mattel* ruling.

Sanctions are different whether they relate to failure to state the reasons or to the contents of the reasoning itself. The lack of reasoning typically entails either the setting aside of the award (e.g. ICSID Convention), or remanding the case back to the arbitral tribunal so that the omission may be put right and the reasons given. The latter is the current solution under English Law pursuant to Art. 70(4) of the 1996 Arbitration Act).[18]

The substance of the reasons given might lead to the award being set aside when the outcome would be contrary to public policy but this sanction is not always applied. For instance, awards tainted by corruption will only be annulled on grounds of Public Policy under Swiss Law in the event that the reasons set out in the award show that the arbitrators chose wilfully to turn a blind eye to issues of corruption.

VI. CONCLUSION

My conclusion is that, at the end of the day, the practice of international arbitration shows that the duty to state reasons is generally understood in fairly similar ways across jurisdictions, both in terms of its recognition and ambit. It is as though the wind of practical exigencies has erased the footprints on the various routes taken by arbitrators during their training to leave but a single path. But may each one of us proceed at his own pace!

NOTES

1. Lord Justice Gordon Hewart, *The King v Sussex Justices,* (1923): "It is not merely of some importance but it is fundamental importance that justice should not only be done, but should manifestly and undoubtedly be seen to be done".
2. Accursius, *Digests*, 11, 6, 1. See P. Taxier, "Jalons pour une histoire de la motivation des sentences", in *La motivation, Travaux de l'Association H. Capitant,* LGDJ, 1998, p. 5, esp. p. 8.
3. See P. Taxier, *op. cit.,* p. 12.
4. See J.-L. Delvolvé, "Essai sur la motivation des sentences arbitrales", *Revue de l'arbitrage,* 1989, p. 149, esp. p. 155-156.
5. See S. Sanchez Lorenzo, "Un análisis comparado de la motivación del laudo en el arbitraje comercial internacional ", in *Arbitraje: Revista de Arbitraje comercial y de inversiones,* 2018, vol. 11, p. 659.
6. Lord Mansfield, quoted by the Rt. Hon. Lord Justice Bingham, "Reasons and reasons for reasons: differences between a Court judgment and an arbitral award", *Arb. Int.,* 1988, p. 141.
7. D. Jousse, "Traité de l'administration de la Justice", t. II, 1771 p. 34: "It is not necessary for the Judges to express the reason for their decisions (...) But, should they so wish, it is up to them. However, it is best not to give the reasons, in order to avoid any bickering by the losing party". Talleyrand: "Never explain the reasons for your decision: the decision might be right and the reasons wrong".
8. See the detailed comparative study done by S. Sanchez Lorenzo, *op. cit.*
9. Art. 48.3 and the sanction of this obligation under art. 52.1.e ; *adde*, art. 47.1.i et 50.1.c.iii of the arbitration rules.
10. Lord Bingham, *op. cit.,* p. 145.
11. See Ch. Jarrosson, "L'acceptabilité de la sentence", *Revue de l'arbitrage,* 2012, p. 793.
12. Cour de cassation, Chambre mixte, 6 September 2002, *Bull. n° 4.*
13. Court of Appeal, *Lord Denning MR, Ward v James* [1966] 1 Q.B. 273.; 1 *Lloyds Rep.* 145.
14. Arrêt *Elmassian*, Cass. civ. 1, 14 June 1960, *Rev. crit. DIP,* 1960, p. 393 and Ph. Francescakis, p. 297: the lack of reasoning in an English award is not, in itself, an infringement of French International Public Policy. This remains an obligation that one might exceptionally be exempted of as long as equivalent guaranties have been secured. See, H. Motulsky, "Le droit naturel dans la pratique jurisprudentielle: le respect des droits de la défense en procédure civile", *Mélanges Roubier,* 1961, t. 2, p. 175 et *Ecrits, T. I, Etudes et notes de procédure,* Dalloz, p. 60.
15. Cour d'appel de Paris (Pôle 1 - Ch. 1), 2 April 2019, *M. Vincent J. Ryan, sociétés Schooner Capital et Atlantic Investment Partners LLC c/ République de Pologne, Revue de l'arbitrage,* 2019, p. 304 : original text : " L'exigence de motivation des décisions de justice est un élément du droit à un procès équitable. Les arbitres qui s'abstiennent de motiver leur décision méconnaissent l'étendue de leur mission et la reconnaissance d'une sentence dépourvue de motif heurte la conception française de l'ordre public international".
16. Paris Court of Appeal (Pôle 1, Ch. 1), 18 June 2019, Qatar: "failure to state reasons in an award does not open the way to annulment proceedings under French International arbitration law, which means that, besides the violation of international Public Policy, not invoked in this case in point, or a disregard of the principle of due process, the reasoning of the award eludes the supervision of the annulment judge". Original text: "le défaut de motivation d'une sentence n'est pas un cas d'ouverture du recours en annulation dans le droit français de l'arbitrage international, de sorte qu'en dehors des cas de violation de l'ordre public international, non invoquée en l'espèce, ou de méconnaissance du principe de la contradiction, la motivation de la sentence échappe au contrôle du juge de l'annulation."
17. This case-law is assessed in different ways. V. *pro* : E. Gaillard, commentary of Cass. civ. 1, 11 May 1999 et Paris, 26 Oct. 1999, *Revue de l'arbitrage,* 1999, p. 811.; H. Lécuyer, commentary of Cass. civ. 1, 14 June 2000 et Paris, 28 juin June et 16 Nov. 2000, *Revue de l'arbitrage,* 2001 p. 729 ; *contra* : Ch. Seraglini et J. Ortscheidt, "Droit de l'arbitrage interne et international", Montchrestien ed., 2013, n° 546 ; *adde*, A. Mourre, "Réflexions critiques sur la suppression du contrôle de la motivation des sentences arbitrales en droit français", *Bull. ASA,* 2001, vol. 19, Issue 4, p. 634.
18. Relating to the benefit of sending back the award in order to avoid having the said award set aside, see Ch. Jarrosson,"Réflexions sur les sanctions applicables aux sentences arbitrales", in *Liber amicorum Pierre Mayer,* LGDJ, p. 331, esp. §§ 28-29.

Chapter 2

Judicial Review and Reasoning of Arbitral Awards

Perspectives from Africa and the Arab World

by Mohamed Salah Abdel Wahab*

I. INTRODUCTION: DECONSTRUCTING REASONING OF ARBITRAL AWARDS

Reasoning is a fundamental cornerstone of arbitral awards, and legal systems, including civil and common law, provide for the reasoning of awards and judicial decisions.[1] Legal reasoning as a process is perceived as a tool of reasonable persuasion under the compelling force of acceptable arguments.[2]

There is indeed a connection between rhetoric, persuasion and legal reasoning which can be well illustrated in arbitral case law. It has been mentioned that "categorization, narrative, and rhetorics [are] the stuff of everyday life in the law."[3] Aristotle defines rhetoric as "an ability, in each [particular] case, to see the available means of persuasion."[4] In rhetorical argumentation, the premises of the arguments need only be acceptable to the audience that is intended to be convinced.[5]

It is in this context that reasoning may be seen as a means to persuade the recipients and readers of arbitral awards of the existence of a specific process followed in the interpretation and application of the law to established facts in order to reach a certain conclusion.

It is unequivocal that, unless otherwise agreed (subject to any mandatory rules under the *lex loci arbitri* and/or the lex loci executionis), arbitral awards include section(s) on reasoning of the tribunal's determination of the issues in dispute. Thus, reasoning is not a vague requirement, and thus the approach, methodology and scope of reasoning should be carefully considered.[6] Moreover, a high degree of adequacy and clarity in the reasoning of arbitral awards is an assurance that the decision is grounded in the law.[7]

Given the quintessential nature of reasoning and the importance thereof for the integrity and survival of the arbitral award, this article shall address the following topics pertinent to the reasoning of awards: (a) reasoning as a fundamental requisite of awards; (b) the scope, limits and categories of reasoning of awards; (c) reasoning as a ground for judicial review of awards in Africa and in the Arab world; and (d) concluding remarks on the reasoning of awards.

* Chair of Private International Law and Professor of International Arbitration, Cairo University; Founding Partner and Head of International Arbitration, Zulficar & Partners

II. REASONING: A FUNDAMENTAL REQUISITE OF ARBITRAL AWARDS IN AFRICAN AND ARAB LAWS?

Reasoning of arbitral awards is a controversial topic across the globe. It becomes even more controversial when the scope and approach to "reasoning" is discussed. Almost all institutional rules provide basic references to reasoning of awards,[8] and national arbitration laws are no exception, where references to the reasoning of awards are made.

Under this section, I intend to analyse and provide an overview of the reasoning requirement in certain African and Arab states. The general rule is that while States may not differ on the requirement of reasoning of arbitral awards, they do differ regarding the mandatory (or non-mandatory) nature of this requirement, its scope, limits as well as the diverse approaches to reasoning.

For the purpose of the overview and analysis under this section, I intend to address the requisite requirement of reasoning under (a) certain UNCITRAL Model Law ("ML") jurisdictions; and (b) the Uniform Arbitration Act in OHADA jurisdictions.

II.A. The UNCITRAL Model Law and Certain African-Arab Jurisdictions

It is unequivocal that the ML has a far-reaching global influence, as it constitutes the source code for many arbitration laws in diverse jurisdictions. In the context of reasoning, the ML provides an overarching principle in Article 32(2) which reads:

> The award shall state the reasons upon which it is based, unless the parties have agreed that no reasons are to be given or the award is an award on agreed terms under article 30.

Thus, the ML provides for a balanced party autonomy oriented approach to reasoning that is premised on a default rule for reasoning with a possible opt-out mechanism in accordance with the principle of *pacta sunt servanda*.

This ML approach is adopted in many jurisdictions, sometimes with a narrow or broad scope of exceptions. For example, in **Bahrain**, which is a ML-based jurisdiction, Article 31(1) of the Bahraini Arbitration Law (2015) mirrors Article 32(2) of the ML. Similarly, in **Egypt**, Article 43(2) of the Egyptian Arbitration Law (1994) provides that awards should be reasoned, save in cases where (i) the parties agreed otherwise; or (ii) if the law applicable to the arbitral proceedings does not require reasoning. This is exactly the same position adopted in **Syria** under Article 42(3) of the Syrian Arbitration Law (2008), in **Oman** under Article 43(2) of the Omani Arbitration Law (1997), and in the **UAE** under Article 41(4) of the UAE Federal Arbitration Law (2018).

In **Jordan**, the Jordanian Arbitration Law (2001) adopted the same approach to reasoning that is applicable under the Egyptian, Omani, Syrian and UAE arbitration laws. However, following the amendments introduced to the Jordanian Arbitration Law in 2018, Article 41(b) of the 2018 amendments now provides that arbitral awards must be reasoned and no specific exception is listed.

In **Qatar**, which new arbitration law is also ML based, the position is slightly different as Article 31(2) of the Qatari Arbitration Law (2017) provides for three exceptions to reasoning: (i) the parties' agreement; (ii) a consent award on agreed terms; and (iii) the applicable legal rules do not require reasoning. Conversely, in Saudi Arabia, the new Saudi Arbitration Law (2012) lists no exceptions to the reasoning requirement. Article 42(1) of the Saudi Arbitration Law refers to the requirement that arbitral awards must be reasoned.

In **Tunisia**, the law distinguishes between domestic and international arbitrations. The domestic awards must be reasoned and no listed exceptions are mentioned in Article 30 of the Tunisian Arbitration Law (1993). However, in international arbitration, Article 75 of the Tunisian Arbitration Law follows the ML approach, where reasoning may be exceptionally disregarded based on the parties' agreement or in case of an award by consent.

In certain countries in Sub-Saharan Africa the situation merits a mention. In **Mozambique** Article 39(3) of the Mozambican Arbitration Law (1999) mirrors the rule enshrined in Article 32(2) of the ML. This is the same position adopted in **Nigeria** under Article 26 of the Nigerian Arbitration Act (2004), in **Kenya** under Article 31 of the Kenyan Arbitration Act (1995), and in **Zambia** under Section 16 of the Zambian Arbitration Act (2000).

In **Ghana**, Article 49(3)(c) of the Ghanaian Arbitration Law (2010) only refers to the parties' agreement as an exception to the reasoning of awards. In **Angola**, the Angolan Arbitration Law (2003), which is largely based on the Portuguese Arbitration Law (1986), provides for a general rule on reasoning, but Article 27(2) of the Angolan Arbitration Law provides for three exceptions: (i) the parties' agreement to exclude reasoning; (ii) the parties' settlement of their dispute (i.e. award by consent); and/or (iii) the withdrawal of the case.

In **South Africa**, its new International Arbitration Act (2017) follows the ML approach. Article 6 of the Act states: "The Model Law applies in the Republic subject to the provisions of this Act." Article 31 of the Act mirrors Article 32(2) of the ML. Domestic arbitration remains governed by the Arbitration Act (1965) and reasoning is required unless the parties agree otherwise.

II.B. The OHADA Uniform Arbitration Act Approach

The Organization for Harmonization of Business Law in Africa ("OHADA") enacted uniform acts within the OHADA area, among which is the OHADA new Arbitration Law (2017) which entered into force in 2018. The importance of OHADA is that its laws bind all 17 member States and apply notwithstanding any contrary domestic law.[9] The OHADA countries are: **Benin, Burkina Faso, Cameroon, Central African Republic, Comoros, Congo, Ivory Coast, Gabon, Guinea, Guinea Bissau, Equatorial Guinea, Mali, Niger, DR Congo, Senegal, Chad,** and **Togo.**[10]

That said the OHADA Uniform Arbitration Act considers reasoning a fundamental requisite for arbitral awards and the lack thereof may constitute a ground for annulment. Article 20 of the Uniform Act reads in pertinent part:

> The arbitration award shall contain:
> - [...]
> - Reasons upon which the award is based shall be given.

Article 26 of the Uniform Act also states in pertinent part that:

> Recourse for nullity is only admissible in the following cases:
> - [...]
> - if no reasons are given for the award.

Based on the above, it appears that reasoning is a fundamental requisite among the OHADA States and that the absence thereof may lead to nullity under the Uniform Arbitration Act.

III. THE REASONING OF ARBITRAL AWARDS: SCOPE, CHARACTERISTICS, CATEGORIES AND LIMITS—THE CHECKS AND BALANCES

As mentioned above, reasoning remains a fundamental requisite for arbitral awards; its importance transcends its purpose, as it contributes to the legitimacy of the arbitration process and enables losing parties to understand why they lost and how the arbitrators reached their conclusions objectively, neutrally and on the basis of the case record and the governing legal norms.

That said, this section aims at shedding some light on the scope, characteristics, categories and limits of reasoning in a comparative context, in hope of ascertaining the commonalities and differences that define the parameters of arbitral awards in the jurisdictions addressed.

III.A. Scope and Characteristics of Reasoning

Despite the fundamental role and nature of reasoning, the term "reasoning" *per se* varies, to different degrees, from one jurisdiction to another depending on the specific philosophy adopted by the pertinent legal system. For example, jurisdictions that allow appeals on law or the merits, will expect broader and more detailed "reasoning" than those that do not allow any form of appeal. Additionally, jurisdictions differ in their perceptions of the concept of justice and the effect of reasoned award on the parties and their right to be heard.[11]

In Egypt, the Egyptian Arbitration Law does not elaborate on the adequacy of reasoning and does not require a specific form of reasoning of arbitral awards. Article 43 of the Egyptian Arbitration Law provides that an award must include the following: (1) the names and addresses of the parties in dispute, (2) names, addresses, standing and nationalities of the arbitrators, (3) copy of the arbitration agreement, (4) summary of the parties' claims, statements and documents, (5) dispositive of the award, (6) the date and place where the award was issued, (7) the reasoning of the award if required.[12]

While the Egyptian Arbitration Law provides no criteria or elaboration on the content, scope, categories and limits of reasoning of arbitral awards, jurisprudence reveals that it is sufficient to include in the award the legal and factual grounds, which the arbitrators have relied upon when rendering its award,[13] as well as the parties' claims, defences, relief and the arbitrators' analysis and response thereto.[14]

In addition, courts have held that reasons must be sufficient to carry the arbitral award, otherwise the award would be null and void.[15] In this regard, sufficient reasons are: (1) those which relate to the subject matter of the dispute, and (2) denote a rational link with the dispositive of the award, and (3) those addressing a fact.[16] In essence, sufficient reasoning necessitates the existence of reasoning that supports the award in all its aspects and parts, which entails that the award should respond to the main claims, defences and allegations of the parties. The Cairo Court of Appeal ruled that:[17]

> [...] whereas the subject matter of the case and what the claimant company relied upon in the arbitral award is that it lacks reasoning, and [...] that the awards must contain the reasons on which it was founded, otherwise they are deemed void. The general principle is that the arbitral award must be reasoned (i.e. including the reasons on which the award was based, and it does not suffice to consider an award reasoned to mention any reasons, but these reasons must include a set of characteristics or conditions which ensures that the legislator's requirement to mention reasons achieves its purpose. The reasoning of the award must be sufficient—which means sufficient to support the award in all its aspects and parts, this is not the case unless the award has responded/addressed—whether accepting or rejecting—the main claims and allegations of the parties as well as what is being submitted as fundamental defenses for purpose of sustaining same [...]

In certain other jurisdictions, a more liberal approach to reasoning is adopted. For example, in Syria, the Syrian courts have held that it is sufficient to provide general reasoning that suffices to prove the basis upon which the award is based.[18] Similarly, in Kuwait, Kuwaiti courts differentiate between facts and law with respect to reasoning. On facts, "factual reasoning" has been defined as the reasons that justify the identified fact, and only this kind of reasoning may lead to the annulment of the award. However, "legal reasoning" can be defined as the reasons that justify the application of the legal rule chosen to govern the facts of the case, and this type of reasoning does not impact the annulment of the award.[19] This is contrary to the approach of Egyptian courts which have set aside an arbitral award on the basis that a tribunal has applied the Egyptian civil law instead of the Egyptian administrative law.[20]

Moreover, certain jurisdictions have also distinguished arbitral and judicial reasoning, so that what is required for judgments is not necessarily required for awards.[21]

In light of the above, one can distil certain characteristics for the reasoning of arbitral awards:

a) reasons must be specific and clear;

b) reasons must cover the claim, defences and relief sought by the parties; it does not suffice to include reasons for only part of the claim that has been adjudicated.[22] However, it is not required that specific and separate reasons be allocated to each and every aspect of a claim or argument;[23]

c) reasons must purposively establish a rational link with the dispositive and must not be ambiguous;[24]

d) reasons should be persuasive, consistent, rational[25] and rooted in the evidence on record and grounded in the legal norms governing the merits;

e) reasons are not expected or required to address or examine every statement, document or argument advanced by the parties, but must address the claims, defences and arguments that are material to the outcome of the case.

f) reasons must not be contradictory so as to cancel each other, otherwise the award could be set aside, if the contradiction is of such magnitude so as to collapse the basis of the reasoning.[26]

III.B. Categories of Reasoning of Arbitral Awards

Irrespective of the reasoning requirement and its scope and characteristics, there are various categories of reasoning that merit a mention, the most notable of which, for the purpose of this article, are: (a) factual and legal reasoning; and (b) narrow and extended reasoning.

III.B.1. Factual and Legal Reasoning

Distinction between matters of fact and law is not always easy and discernible, as is the case of distinguishing matters of substance and procedure in private international law.[27] The importance of this distinction is twofold: (i) in certain jurisdictions, only the lack or insufficient factual reasoning can give rise to nullity;[28] and (ii) in certain jurisdictions, iura novit arbiter enables arbitral tribunals to engage in more extensive legal reasoning beyond the limits of legal authorities submitted by the parties.

III.B. 2. Narrow and Extended Reasoning

Given that reasoning shapes and informs the decision-making process, it is submitted that the arbitral tribunal's approach to reasoning may likely impact its findings and conclusions. Moreover, whether the tribunal engages in narrow or extensive reasoning may be informed by the nature of the dispute, the parties' expectations, the applicable procedural rules and the governing legal norms.

On a different note, extended or extensive reasoning may either increase the risk of setting aside or challenges against arbitral awards,[29] or ring-fence the award against nullity or challenges. Thus, extensive or extended reasoning is a double-edged sword that is much dependent on the skilful drafting of arbitral tribunals.

Skilled and experienced tribunals would assess the situation and the approach to reasoning on a case-by-case basis in light of the nature of the dispute, the parties' expectations, the applicable procedural rules and the governing legal norms, and in due consideration of the fact that nowadays complex relationships and dispute do call for sufficiently detailed reasoning that affords the parties an adequate opportunity to understand and appreciate the basis and rationale for the tribunal's decisions.

III.C. The Limits of Reasoning of Arbitral Awards

It is submitted that reasoning is not a goal in itself, but is a means to an end, that is: rendering a valid and enforceable award that determines the issues in dispute between the parties. When fulfilling their role, arbitrators, as a general rule, should limit their decision-making process to the facts presented by the parties, their claims, counterclaims and defences, if any.[30]

As highlighted herein, reasoned awards are intended to (i) provide assurances regarding the nature and quality of justice that is being served by the arbitrator;[31] (ii) provide the parties with a satisfactory explanation of the arbitrators' decision and may therefore increase the likelihood of voluntary compliance, since the losing party will feel fully "heard";[32] and (iii) enhance the legitimacy of the arbitral process, even if awards are not reviewed on the merits.[33]

In any event, the arbitrators' reasoning need not go beyond that which was pleaded, argued, claimed and submitted on record. It is in this respect that English courts have held that:[34]

> All that is necessary is that the arbitrators should set out what, on their view of the evidence did or did not happen and should explain succinctly why, in the light of what happened, they have reached their decision and what that decision is. This is all that is meant by a reasoned award.

However, while the position regarding the facts and "factual reasoning" may be clear, such that arbitrators cannot go beyond the facts on record, the position is more controversial regarding "legal reasoning". This brings into question the limits of legal reasoning and whether the principle of iura novit curia, which prevails in certain jurisdictions (primarily of a civil law background), may apply in the context of arbitration, such that the variant principle of iura novit arbiter may enable arbitrators to stretch the limits of legal reasoning.

In a nutshell, under certain legal systems, the principle of iura novit curia or iura novit arbiter may apply, such that arbitrators would not be strictly bound by the parties' submissions on legal issues.[35] The challenge is that national arbitration laws and institutional rules infrequently address the extent to which arbitrators may ex officio ascertain and apply, *sua sponte*, the contents of the lex causae. Subject to few exceptions, national laws and rules do not regulate the means through which the task of ascertaining the contents of the applicable laws and rules is fulfilled and to what extent the powers of arbitral tribunals can be stretched in this regard.

A comparative overview of legal systems within Africa and the Arab world reveals that: (a) the expectation is that parties are generally responsible for ascertaining the content of the applicable substantive law; and (b) arbitrators enjoy a discretionary power to research the law and raise legal issues *sua sponte*. This has even been the subject to several recommendations by the ILA. In its Final Report,[36] the ILA stated the following:

> [...]
>
> 5. Arbitrators should primarily receive information about the contents of the applicable law from the parties.
>
> 6. In general, and subject to Recommendation 13, arbitrators should not introduce legal issues—propositions of law that may bear on the outcome of the dispute—that the parties have not raised.
>
> 7. Arbitrators are not confined to the parties' submissions about the contents of applicable law. Subject to Recommendation 8, arbitrators may question the parties about legal issues the parties have raised and about their submissions and evidence on the contents of the applicable law, may review sources not invoked by the parties relating to those legal issues and may, in a transparent manner rely, on their own knowledge as to the applicable law as it relates to those legal issues.

> 8. Before reaching their conclusions and rendering a decision or an award, arbitrators should give parties a reasonable opportunity to be heard on legal issues that may be relevant to the disposition of the case. They should not give decisions that might reasonably be expected to surprise the parties, or any of them, or that are based on legal issues not raised by or with the parties.

However, the arbitrators' authority to raise legal issues *sua sponte* with the parties in view of addressing same in their reasoning is neither absolute nor unconstrained. The arbitrators' authority is subject to the overarching principle of due process such that arbitrators may not take the parties by surprise when applying the law or reasoning their awards. The parameters of arbitrators' authority to apply the principle of iura novit arbiter (which remains subject to the "no surprise" restriction) are a fertile terra nova for arbitral scholarship and jurisprudence.

By and large, it should be noted that, when exercising their authority and discretion in addressing legal issues and the related legal reasoning, arbitrators remain subject to three essential constraints: (a) ne ultra petita, (b) transparency and foreseeability, and (c) due process (as inclusive of the right to be heard).[37]

Thus, there are indeed limits to reasoning of arbitral awards, such that the arbitrators are expected to (i) consider, review and assess the facts and evidence on record; (ii) address what did and did not happen regarding the issues in dispute; (iii) explain how and why they have reached their decision(s); (iv) avoid surprising the parties regarding issues of law or fact that neither party raised and/or either party had no opportunity to address; and (v) measure with precision the degree, extent and scope of reasoning that adequately and sufficiently support their decision(s), without engaging in unnecessary extended reasoning or deficient and incomplete reasoning.

IV. JUDICIAL REVIEW OF ARBITRAL AWARDS IN AFRICA AND THE ARAB WORLD: THE REASONING CHALLENGE AND CHALLENGED REASONING

Judicial review and enforcement of arbitral awards in African and Arab jurisdictions remain topical issues and a fertile land for scrutiny. In the specific context of reasoning of awards, several principles are at play: (a) party autonomy and *pacta sunt servanda*; (b) finality and *res judicata* of awards; and (c) non-review of arbitral awards on the merits. The relative equilibrium between these principles and the judicial approach to reasoning in a specific legal system determines the balance that African courts strike when reviewing the reasoning of arbitral awards in the context of setting aside or enforcement proceedings.

While arbitration is an inherently autonomy driven process and a consent oriented mechanism for settlement of disputes, such autonomy and consent do not operate within a vacuum, but exist within the realm of legal systems and territorial jurisdictions. These legal systems and jurisdictions do limit their review of awards to that which is determined to be necessary to strike a balance between the competing interests of finality and justice. African arbitration laws generally provide for a set of limited grounds upon which a reviewing court may vacate or decline to enforce an arbitral award.

In Africa and the Arab world, extensive judicial review of arbitral awards is in regress and amity towards arbitration is generally on the rise, despite certain jurisdictional set-backs. African and Arab States, as is the case with countries in other regions of the world, are witnessing a profound transmogrification towards supporting credible arbitration proceedings. This is indeed a notable trend despite the exceptional temporary set-backs in few jurisdictions.[38]

Many African and Arab States have ratified the New York Convention on the Recognition and Enforcement of Foreign Arbitral Awards (1958) and have enacted new UNCITRAL Model Law-based legislation and/or modernized their arbitration laws and legislative framework to align Africa with international practices. That said, *de novo* judicial review of the merits and the review of arbitral awards on the substance are unwelcomed on the Continent. This is a notable trend in North and Sub-Saharan Africa as well as in the Gulf region.[39]

As detailed herein above, whether jurisdictions that have adopted the Model Law or jurisdictions within which the OHADA Uniform Arbitration Act applies, the prevailing principle is that the grounds for review of awards are limited and reasoning features as a ground insofar as the parties or the local law did not require reasoning. Thus, it is submitted that reasoning itself presents a challenge to courts when reviewing awards and, at the same time, awards may be challenged on the basis of lack of reasoning absent a consent by the parties or an express legal provision dispensing with the need for reasoning.

By way of example, in **Egypt**, while reasoning is required as a matter of law unless (i) the parties have dispensed with the reasoning requirement by consent; (ii) a specific law dispenses with reasoning; and/or (iii) the award is an award by consent or on agreed terms, the prevailing judicial trends have confirmed that "insufficient reasoning" is not sufficient to set aside or deny the enforcement of an award. Only "lack of reasoning" qualifies as a ground for setting aside or refusal of recognition and enforcement. This is the practice of the Cairo Court of Appeal which, in various circuits, has held that:

> contradiction in the reasons of an award is not considered one of the grounds/causes for the annulment provided for in Article 53 of the Arbitration Law [...], because this reason of annulment is a subjective one does not encompass the rehearsal/reconsideration of the subject matter of the dispute. [...][40]

And

> [...] it is established that the discretion of the court ruling over the annulment of the arbitral award does not extend to reviewing the award, and assess its appropriateness, or observing the proper evaluation of the arbitrators [....], or the sufficiency of the reasoning of the award for its convey or deficiencies, as the court of annulment does not have power to review these issues as it is not a court of appeal for the arbitral award.[...][41]

In **Nigeria**, Section 26(3)(a) of the ACA (Arbitration and Conciliation Act 1988) states that "the arbitral tribunal shall state on the award [...] the reasons upon which it is based, unless the **parties have agreed that no reasons** are to be given or the award is an **award on agreed terms** [...]", and Nigerian courts have not placed significant limitations on the reasoning of awards beyond what is stated in the Act. However, the case of *Tettrazini Foods Limited v Abbacon Investment Ltd.* & Anor (2015) LPELR-25007(CA) provides very helpful insights into the Nigerian courts' approach to judicial review of reasoning. The Nigerian Court of Appeal held that:

> A reasoned award was defined in the case of *Bremer Handelsgesellschaft mbH v Westzucker GmbH* (No. 2) (1981) 2 Lloyds Rep. 130 at 132-133 thus:
>
> "All that is necessary is that the arbitrators should set out what, on their view of the evidence did or did not happen and should explain succinctly why, in the light of what happened, they have reached their decision and what that decision is. This is all that is meant by a reasoned award."
>
> From the foregoing, a **reasoned award** must include the following:
>
> a) Set out the **evidence led by the parties**.
>
> b) Set out **what did or did not happen** as between the parties to the arbitral proceedings.
>
> c) **Explain why, in the light of what happened, the arbitrators have reached their decision**, and
>
> d) State what the decision is.
>
> Looking at the award made by the 2nd Respondent, it is obvious that it **lacks the evidence** set out by the parties, the **strength and failures of each side, no explanation of what happened and how the decision was arrived at**, i.e. from what items of the contract. I**t is therefore clear that the award failed to include the elements required to make the award a reasoned award.** This is a breach of the requirement of law and that is also a misconduct. I agree that **the award is not expected to be like a court judgment but all that is required is a mention of the required elements to make it a reasoned award.** [42] [Emphasis added]

Thus, arbitrators shall render their award with balanced factual and legal reasoning, so that the reviewing court is able to review same for the purpose of any challenge or enforcement. That is why all African and Arab countries require an arbitral award to include the reasons upon which it is based,[43] and some countries excluded such obligation only in cases where the parties have agreed otherwise, or where the applicable law to the arbitral proceedings does not require reasons to be given.[44] Other laws have expressly referred to non-reasoning when the award is rendered on agreed terms (i.e. awards by consent).[45]

However, it has been suggested that courts when reviewing the reasoning of arbitral awards should consider that they are distinct from court judgments,[46] especially that court judgments are normally reviewed on both facts and law and could be subject to an appeal, whereas arbitral awards are not normally reviewed on the merits and not subject to appeal, unless the applicable lex loci arbitri so provides.[47]

The annulment of the arbitral awards resulting from the absence of reasoning or reasoning related issues is not always expressed legislatively. However, some laws explicitly provide that annulment is the penalty for lack of reasoning,[48] or for contradictions in the reasoning.[49]

That said, from among the trends pertaining to the annulment of arbitral awards and the challenges brought against requests or orders for recognition and enforcement of awards in Africa and the Arab world, one may distil the following judicial trends with respect to reasoning:[50]

a) absence of reasoning (save in cases where (i) parties agreed to dispense with reasoning or requested consent awards and/or (ii) the lex loci arbitri does not require reasoning) is a ground for setting aside or refusal of enforcement and recognition in almost all jurisdictions within Africa or the Arab world;

b) contradictions in reasoning and/or insufficient reasoning is not subject to a uniform rule, while certain jurisdictions do not consider this to be a ground for setting aside or refusal of recognition and enforcement (unless such contradictions are manifest to the extent that they cancel the reasons or render the reasoning inexistent) as is the case in Egypt, other jurisdictions consider contradictory or insufficient reasoning a ground for setting aside or refusal of recognition and enforcement;[51]

c) awards are generally not reviewed on the merits and a reviewing court may not, in principle, check the correctness of the reasoning of the arbitrators as is the case in Egypt and Lebanon;[52] yet, in few jurisdictions, manifestly wrong legal reasoning may exceptionally qualify as a possible ground for setting aside or refusal of recognition and enforcement as is the case in Ethiopia (in the Supreme Court of Ethiopia (Cassation Bench) judgment of 24 May 2018 regarding the case of *Chemin de Fer Djibouto-Ethiopien v Consta Joint Venture*);[53]

d) arbitrators are generally not obliged to address each and every argument raised by the parties, insofar as their reasoning is sufficiently clear and adequate to address the issues in dispute and the parties' claims and counterclaims such that the losing party and the reviewing court can understand the basis of the arbitrators' determinations;[54] and

e) in jurisdictions that adopt iura novit arbiter arbitrators are not barred from raising legal issues sua sponte with the parties in view of addressing same in their reasoning. However, the arbitrators' authority is subject to three essential constraints: (a) ne ultra petita, (b) transparency and foreseeability, and (c) due process (as inclusive of the right to be heard).

V. CONCLUSION RECONSTRUCTING REASONING OF AWARDS—PRESENT PROSPECTS AND FUTURE TRENDS

International arbitration is destined to be the premier choice for the resolution of business disputes. However, in order for arbitration to retain its position, legitimacy and status, and enjoy the trust and confidence of users, awards must continue to exhibit good quality reasoning. A well-drafted and adequately reasoned award is a certificate of excellence and a clear pass to a highly reduced risk of setting aside or refusal of recognition and enforcement.

Nevertheless, drafting a well-reasoned award may prove to be a challenging endeavour and a daunting task, yet this task can be greatly facilitated if the parties cooperate with the arbitrators during the proceedings and when the arbitrators have carefully reviewed the case file, are able to correctly distil the issues in dispute, and have a solid grasp of the fundamental principles underlying the reasoning of awards.

Reasoning is indeed crucial to any award, and, as detailed above, is usually expressly required by many national arbitration laws—and most arbitration rules and Africa and the Arab world are no exception. Reasoning is intended to (i) provide assurances regarding the nature and quality of justice that is being served by the arbitrator;[55] (ii) provide the parties with a satisfactory explanation of the arbitrators' decision and may therefore increase the likelihood of voluntary compliance, since the losing party will feel fully "heard";[56] and (iii) enhance the legitimacy of the arbitral process, even if awards are not reviewed on the merits.[57]

As stated in the IBA Toolkit for Award Writing, award reasoning constrains the powers of arbitrators by compelling them to base their decision(s) on the law and facts on record and it reduces the risk of arbitrary decision-making.[58] The Toolkit goes on to emphasize the need for sufficient reasoning and expressly states:[59]

One way to ensure sufficient reasoning is to refer closely to the list of dispositive issues (as agreed by the parties or determined by the arbitral tribunal) and to address each of the parties' main arguments on each issue. With regard to the dispositive issues, the award should explain the reasoning according to which the arbitral tribunal applied the applicable law to the relevant facts (including references to the factual record).

As stated above, arbitrators should keep in mind that awards are first and foremost written for the parties and primarily for the losing party; the more solid, clear and adequate the reasoning is, the more likely it will be accepted and the less likely the award will be challenged and set aside or denied enforcement and recognition by any reviewing court.

A survey of the leading African and Arab jurisdictions reveals that reasoning is critical to any arbitral award and that reviewing courts are exceedingly taking a measured approach to reasoning, that is founded on prudent equilibrium between the principles of party autonomy, finality, non-review of awards on the merits and the necessity for clear, adequate and solid reasoning to ring-fence awards against successful challenges.

However, it has been seen that the scope, characteristics, categories and limits of reasoning are not always well defined and addressed legislatively in jurisdictions across the globe, including African and Arab jurisdictions. Nevertheless, it is submitted that among the notable and desired characteristics for the reasoning of arbitral awards are: (i) clarity, cogency, consistency, completeness, specificity and rationality; (ii) being rooted in the evidence on record and grounded in the legal norms governing the merits; (iii) addressing the claims, defences and arguments that are material to the outcome of the case; and (iv) not being overly extended or unwarrantedly narrowed.

That said, arbitrators are not expected to be arbitrary when it comes to reasoning and their authority and powers are not freed from the shackles of legal wisdom, such that arbitrators are expected to: (i) consider, review and assess the facts and evidence on record; (ii) address what did and did not happen regarding the issues in dispute; (iii) explain how and why they have reached their decision(s); (iv) avoid surprising the parties regarding issues of law or fact that neither party raised and/or either party had no opportunity to address; and (v) measure with precision the degree, extent and scope of reasoning that adequately and sufficiently support their decision(s), without engaging in unnecessary extended reasoning or deficient and incomplete reasoning.

Moreover, it has been seen that in Africa and the Arab world, extensive judicial review of arbitral awards is in regress and amity towards arbitration is generally on the rise, despite certain jurisdictional set-backs. Furthermore, it is submitted that courts when reviewing the reasoning of arbitral awards should consider that they are not court judgments that can be reviewed on both facts and law, and so several judicial trends with respect to reasoning were considered and addressed.

By and large, the reasoning of awards in African and Arab jurisdictions is generally aligned with best practices internationally, noting that reasoning of awards remains at the heart of the legitimacy of the arbitral process and central to its success. Moreover, courts in African and Arab jurisdictions are increasingly becoming experienced and nuanced in their measured review of arbitral awards. It is submitted that (i) as more and more arbitrations proliferate across African and Arab jurisdictions, (ii) as more and more useful information and communication technologies are integrated within the process to assist arbitrators, and (iii) as more and more arbitrators observe the requirements of good reasoning, the less and less awards will be successfully challenged, and more trust and confidence in the process will eclipse isolated incidents of bad reasoning.

NOTES

1. See "Chapter 3: The Dynamics of Reasoning", in Mary Mitsi, "The Decision-Making Process of Investor-State Arbitration Tribunals", *International Arbitration Law Library*, Volume 46, *Kluwer Law International* 2018, pp. 89 –102, available at http://www.kluwerarbitration.com/document/kli-ka-mitsi-2018-ch03?q=%22reasoning%20of%20arbitral%20awards%22. In the common law system, it was common practice for courts to render unreasoned awards except for specialised areas of law such as maritime arbitration. The modern trend is to give reasons for the decisions. See Marta Infantino, "International Arbitral Awards' Reasons: Surveying the State-of-the-Art in Commercial and Investment International Dispute Settlements" (2014) 5 JIDS 175, 175; See also Jerzy Stelmach and Bartosz Brozek, "Methods of Legal Reasoning" (Springer 2006) (the authors analyse the four methods used in legal practice, legal dogmatics and legal theory: logic, analysis, argumentation and hermeneutics).
2. See MacCormick, "Rhetoric and the Rule of Law: A Theory of Legal Reasoning", (n 172), p. 17 et seq, available at https://www.oxfordscholarship.com/view/10.1093/acprof:oso/9780199571246.001.0001/acprof-9780199571246.
3. See Anthony Amsterdam and Jerome Bruner, "Minding the Law", (HUP 2002) 2, available at http://www.hup.harvard.edu/catalog.php?isbn=9780674008168.
4. See Aristotle, "On Rhetoric", (George Kennedy tr, OUP 1991) 36, available at https://issuu.com/bouvard6/docs/aristotle__on_rhetoric__oxf_.
5. See Van Eemeren and Grootendorst, "A Systematic Theory of Argumentation", (n 18) 43, available at https://pdfs.semanticscholar.org/3e38/d3ca665a2cdcb05d806e66aea277b1b0f78a.pdf.
6. See "Chapter 4: The Functions of Reasoning", in Mary Mitsi, "The Decision-Making Process of Investor-State Arbitration Tribunals", *International Arbitration Law Library*, (2018) Volume 46 (*Kluwer Law International*) pp. 103 –116, available at http://www.kluwerarbitration.com/document/kli-ka-mitsi-2018-ch04?q=%22reasoning%20of%20arbitral%20awards%22. See also, Infantino, "International Arbitral Awards' Reasons" (n 393) 182. See also, Cheng and Trisotto, "Reasons and Reasoning in Investment Treaty Arbitration" (n 409) 424.
7. ibid. See also, Ortino, "Legal Reasoning of International Investment Tribunals" (n 533) 34.
8. See for example, Articles 31(2) and 32(2) of the 2017 ICC Arbitration Rules.
9. Article 10 of the OHADA Treaty states that the OHADA Uniform Acts are directly applicable and binding "[...] notwithstanding any contrary provision of the domestic law, be it anterior or posterior [...]"

10. See State Members of OHADA, available at https://www.ohada.org/index.php/en/centrafrique/ centrafrique-at-a-glance.
11. See S.I. Strong, "Reasoned Awards in International Commercial Arbitration", available at http://arbitrationblog.kluwerarbitration.com/2016/02/19/reasoned-awards-in-international-commercial-arbitration/.
12. See also: Fathi Waly, "Arbitration in National and International Commercial Dispute in Practice and Theory", 2014 ed., pages 555-567; Judge Maher Abou Al-Enien, "*Adjudication of Arbitration*", Vol. 2, pages 40-49; Mahmoud Salama, *Encyclopedia of Arbitration and Arbitration*, 2009 ed., pages 377 and 378; The Cairo Court of Appeal, Case No. 100 of Judicial Year No. 122, Hearing Session dated 6 January 2009.
13. See Cairo Court of Appeal, Case No. 42 of Judicial Year No. 119, Hearing Session dated 23 January 2002. See also, Judge Maher Abou Al-Enien, *Adjudication of Arbitration*, Vol.2, page 46.
14. See Cairo Court of Appeal, Case No. 61 and 147 of Judicial Year No. 124, Hearing Session dated 2 September 2008. See also, Judge Maher Abou Al-Enien, *Adjudication of Arbitration*, Vol.2, page 46.
15. See Fathi Waly, "Arbitration in National and International Commercial Dispute in Practice and Theory", 2014 ed., pages 754 and 755.
16. ibid. Pages 750 and 755. See also, Cairo Court of Appeal, Case No. 73 of Judicial Year No. 119, Hearing Session dated 6 July 2002.
17. See Cairo Court of Appeal, Case No. 62 of Judicial Year No. 114, Hearing Session dated 6 April 2011. See also, International Arbitration Journal, Vol. 12, 2011, page 693. See also, Cairo Court of Appeal, Case No. 89 of Judicial Year No. 120, Hearing Session dated 28 February 2004.
18. See Syrian Court of Cassation, Decision No. 478, dated 12/3/1988.
19. See Kuwaiti Court of Cassation, Challenge No. 19 of the Year 1987, dated 10 June 1987.
20. See Cairo Court of Appeal, Judgment of 5 December 1995 in the matter concerning Chromalloy Aeroservices and the Arab Republic of Egypt, 939 F. Supp. 906 (D.C. Cir. 1996)
21. See Kuwaiti Court of Cassation, Challenge No. 19 of the Year 1987, dated 10 June 1987; and Kuwaiti Court of Cassation, Challenge No. 144 of the Year 1989, dated 23 October 1989.
22. See Fathi Waly, "Arbitration in National and International Commercial Dispute in Practice and Theory", 2014 ed., page 569.
23. See the Egyptian Court of Cassation, Challenge No. 33 of Judicial Year No. 53, Hearing Session dated 21 March 1988; the Cairo Court of Appeal, Case No. 63 of Judicial Year 126, Hearing Session dated 2 February 2010.
24. See Fathi Waly, "Arbitration in National and International Commercial Dispute in Practice and Theory", 2014 ed., pages 569, 570 and 750; Judge Maher Abou Al-Enien, *Adjudication of Arbitration*, Vol. 2, pages 45-46; The Cairo Court of Appeal, Case No. 73 of Judicial Year No. 119, Hearing Session dated 6 July 2002; Cairo Court of Appeal, Case No. 26 of Judicial Year No. 114, Hearing Session dated 18 February 1998; and Cairo Court of Appeal, Case No. 61 and 147 of Judicial Year No. 124, Hearing Session dated 2 September 2008; and Cairo Court of Appeal, Case No. 13 of Judicial Year No. 128, Hearing Session dated 2 November 2011.
25. See Tunisian Court of Appeal, Decision No. 25, dated 10/2/1998.
26. Fathi Waly, "Arbitration in National and International Commercial Dispute in Practice and Theory", 2014 ed., page 573. See also, Tunisian Court of Appeal, Decision No. 40, dated 4/5/1999.
27. See Mohamed S. Abdel Wahab, "Essays on the General Principles of Private International Law", Vol. 1, 2017; Cairo University Press, page 62 et seq.
28. See Kuwaiti Court of Cassation, Challenge No. 19 of the Year 1987, dated 10 June 1987.
29. Lord Mansfield advised the Governor of an Island in the West Indies (who also sat as a judge):

    > Be of good cheer—take my advice, and you will be reckoned a great judge as well as a great commander-in-chief. Nothing is more easy; only hear both sides patiently—then consider what you think justice requires, and decide accordingly. But never give your reasons; for your judgment will probably be right, but your reasons will certainly be wrong.

    See William Seward, "Anecdotes of Some Distinguished Persons, Chiefly of the Present and Two Preceding Centuries", Vol. II, 3rd ed., 1796 (London), page 386.
30. See Mohamed S. Abdel Wahab, "Iura Novit Arbiter: The Known Unknown", in Festschrift Ahmed Sadek El-Kosheri, *Kluwer Law International* (2015), pp. 3-25; See also, Christian Collantes, "Give Me the Facts and I'll Give You the Law: What Are the Limits of the Iura Novit Arbiter Principle in

International Arbitration?", *Kluwer Law International* (2019), available at http://arbitrationblog.kluwerarbitration.com/2019/01/10/give-me-the-facts-and-ill-give-you-the-law-what-are-the-limits-of-the-iura-novit-arbiter-principle-in-international-arbitration/.

31. See Mohamed Abd Al Raouf, "Analysis Study to the Egyptian Judiciary with respect to the Annulment Cases", *Journal of Arab Arbitration*, Volume 11, June 2008, page 131, fn. 3.

32. See Ashgan Feisal Shoukry Dawood, "The legal nature of the arbitral award, its effects and its challenge manners. Comparative Study", PhD Thesis, 2008, An-Najah National University, Palestine, page 129.

33. See Judge Ismail Ibrahim Al-Zayadi, "The Arbitration and Judiciary Diligence", pages118-119.

34. See *Bremer Handelsgellschaft v Westzucker* (No. 2) (1981) 2 *Lloyds Reports* pages 130 & 132-133.

35. See Mohamed S. Abdel Wahab, "*Iura Novit Arbiter*: The Known Unknown", in Festschrift Ahmed Sadek El-Kosheri, *Kluwer Law International* (2015), pages 3-25; Cezary Wiśniewski, "Who Should Know The Law: The Arbitrators Or The Parties?", *Kluwer Law International* (2016), available at http://arbitrationblog.kluwerarbitration.com/2016/10/03/who-should-know-the-law-the-arbitrators-or-the-parties/.

36. See International Law Association, Final Report on Ascertaining the Contents of the Applicable Law in International Commercial Arbitration (2008), pages 15-16.

37. See Mohamed S. Abdel Wahab, "*Iura Novit Arbiter*: The Known Unknown", in Festschrift Ahmed Sadek El-Kosheri, *Kluwer Law International* (2015), page 24.

38. See Shirley Aggrey Mlimuka, "A Perspective of the Role of Tanzanian National Courts in Commercial Arbitration", available at https://pdfs.semanticscholar.org/bd8c/b90ecee9c365b-4922f87fd6f00bee113ac 88.pdf.

39. For a contrary view regarding a recent trend in Ethiopia, see Mintewab Afework, "The Fate of Finality Clause in Ethiopia" (2018), available at http://arbitrationblog.kluwerarbitration.com/2018/07/22/fate-finality-clause-ethiopia-2/, where the Supreme Court of Ethiopia (Cassation Bench), ruled on 24 May 2018 that it has the power to review the award on "*fundamental error of law grounds*" despite the parties' express agreement on the finality of the arbitral award. This approach, which resonates with the concept of "*manifest disregard of the law*" does impact the review of the reasoning of awards, where the Ethiopian Supreme Court did not only consider the adequacy of the reasoning, but assessed the correctness of the findings on the applicable Ethiopian law. The judgment of 2018 was in relation to the recent arbitral award in the case of the Government of Ethiopia and Djibouti, represented by the *Chemin de Fer Djibouto-Ethiopien ("CDE"), and Consta Joint Venture ("Consta")*, where the majority of the tribunal awarded Consta in excess of 20 million euros and rejected all of CDE's defences and counterclaims, but the Supreme Court of Ethiopia held that it was entitled to review the arbitral award for fundamental errors of Ethiopian law, but it also decided that such errors existed in the case.

40. See Fathy Waly "Arbitration in National and International Commercial Dispute in Practice and Theory", 2014 edn., pages 753, see also Cairo Court of Appeal, case no. 49 of J.Y 120, hearing session 22 November 2003, see also Cairo Court of Appeal, case no. 54 of J.Y 120, hearing session 30 December 2003, see also Cairo Court of Appeal, case no. 89 of J.Y 120, hearing session 28 February 2004.

41. See Cairo Court of Appeal, cases no. 61, 147 of J.Y 124, hearing session 2 September 2008.

42. See Page 2, item 1 and page 20 of the Nigerian Court of Appeal judgment.

43. See for example, the Article 1027 of the 2008 Algerian Law No. 08/09 of Civil and Administrative Procedure; Article 42(1) of the 2012 Saudi Law of Arbitration issued by the Royal Decree No. M/34; Article 34 of the Sudanese Arbitration Act of 2016; Article 39(1) of the Palestinian Law on Arbitration No. 3/2000; Article 183 of the Kuwaiti Law No. 38/1980 of Civil and Commercial Procedure; Article 790(5) of the Lebanese Law No. 90/1983 of the Civil Procedure; and Article 760 of the 1953 Libyan Civil Procedures Law.

44. See for example, Article 43(2) of the Egyptian Arbitration Law No. 27/1994; Article 41(4) of the UAE Federal Arbitration Law No. 06/2018; Articles 265 and 270(2) of the Iraqi Law No. 83/1969 of Civil Procedures; Article 31 of the Bahraini Arbitration Law No. 09/2015; Article 75(2) of the Tunisian Arbitration Law No.42/1993; Article 75(2) of the Syrian Arbitration Law No. 04/2008; Article 43(2) of the Omani Arbitration Law No.47/1997; Article 31(2) of the Qatari Arbitration Law No.02/2017; Article 48 of the Yemeni Arbitration Law No. 22/1992; and Article 57 of the Mauritanian Arbitration Law No. 06/2000.

45. See for example, Section 26(3)(a) of the Nigerian Arbitration and Conciliation Act 1988.

46. See Mohamed Selim Al-Awa, "The Arbitration Law in Egypt and Arab Countries", Part 2, ed. 2014, page 398; Kuwait Court of Cassation (Al-Tameez), Commercial, Case No. 441 of the year

1998; see also, Ashgan Feisal Shoukry Dawood, "The legal nature of the arbitral award, its effects and its challenge manners. Comparative Study", PhD Thesis, 2008, An-Najah National University, Palestine, page 37.

47. See Fathy Waly, "The Arbitration in the National and International Commercial Disputes", 1st ed 2014, page 568.
48. See Article 53 of the Yemeni Arbitration Law No. 22 of the Year 1992, which stipulates: "Without prejudice to the provisions hereof, the avoidance of the award may only be requested in the following cases: [...] (f) if the award was not reasoned; [...]"
49. See Article 769 of the Libyan Civil Procedures Law for the Year 1953 which reads: "Reasons to request the annulment of arbitrators' awards; [...] (4) If the arbitral award dealt with matters not falling within the scope of the arbitration agreement or exceeded the limits of this agreement, or included an explicit contradiction; [...]"
50. See Dr. Fathy Waly, "The Arbitration in the National and International Commercial Disputes", 1st ed. 2014, pages 749-756; See also, Mahmoud Samir Al-Sharkawy, "The International Commercial Arbitration", ed. 2011, pages 512-514.
51. See Tunisian Court of Cassation, Case No. 20596/2007 issued on 21/11/2008.
52. See Egyptian Court of Cassation, Case No. 537 of Judicial Year 73, issued on 2014; see also, Beirut Court of Appeal, 1st Circuit, Case No. 192 of the Year 2011.
53. See Mintewab Afework, "The Fate of Finality Clause in Ethiopia" (2018), available at http://arbitrationblog.kluwerarbitration.com/2018/07/22/fate-finality-clause-ethiopia-2/.
54. See for example, Board of Grievances, Saudi Arabia, Decision of the Court of 1st Instance No. 35/d/tc/2/3, issued in 2012
55. See Mohamed Abd Al Raouf, "Analysis Study to the Egyptian Judiciary with respect to the Annulment Cases", *Journal of Arab Arbitration*, Volume 11, June 2008, page 131, fn. 3.
56. See Ashgan Feisal Shoukry Dawood, "The legal nature of the arbitral award, its effects and its challenge manners. Comparative Study", PhD Thesis, 2008, An-Najah National University, Palestine, page 129.
57. See Judge Ismail Ibrahim Al-Zayadi, "The Arbitration and Judiciary Diligence", pages118 - 119.
58. IBA Arbitration Committee, IBA Toolkit for Award Writing (September 2016), page 37.
59. ibid.

Chapter 3

Legal Reasoning in International Commercial Disputes

Empirically Testing the Common Law-Civil Law Divide

by S.I. Strong*

ABSTRACT

Although legal reasoning is central to the dispute resolution process, very little is actually known about how judges and arbitrators approach that particular task. Instead, anecdotes and assumptions abound, with international disputes suffering the most, due to longstanding but largely unsupported theories about purported differences between common law and civil law reasoning.

This Article provides unique and useful insights into the legal reasoning process by presenting data from a recent large-scale empirical study of legal reasoning in commercial disputes. The discussion begins by considering why judges and arbitrators from common law and civil law countries write reasoned rulings before moving on to analyse and compare the importance of different types of legal authorities in substantive and procedural disputes. In so doing, the Article not only tests empirical findings against various theoretical assumptions relating to legal reasoning but also identifies the extent to which common law and civil law respondents diverge in their beliefs and practice. The analysis closes with a discussion of how providers of judicial and arbitral education can assist common law and civil law judges and arbitrators seeking to improve the way they approach legal reasoning.

I. INTRODUCTION

One of the hallmarks of international commercial arbitration involves the routine use of fully reasoned awards, a phenomenon that makes international commercial arbitration comparable to litigation in terms of complexity, sophistication and nuance.[1] However, very little information exists as to what constitutes a reasoned award in the international commercial context,[2] how international commercial awards differ from judicial decisions (if at all) and whether and to what extent any distinctions in legal reasoning arise across the common law-civil law divide.[3]

This final item is of particular interest, both as a scholarly and a practical matter, given the purposeful blend of common law and civil law elements and the predominance of both common law and civil law arbitrators in international commercial arbitration. This Article therefore seeks to provide tangible insights into longstanding questions about the nature and quality

* Associate Professor of Law, University of Sydney

of legal reasoning in commercial disputes by testing longstanding theoretical assumptions about alleged differences between common law and civil law reasoning against recently published empirical research. In so doing, this Article not only improves individual and institutional understanding of current practices in the field but also offers tangible suggestions on how the arbitral community might move forward in light of that knowledge.

The discussion proceeds as follows. First, section II sets forth the theoretical justification for fully reasoned awards, looking at best practices in both common law and civil law jurisdictions. Those assumptions are then tested empirically, using data generated from a recent large-scale study of legal reasoning in commercial disputes. Next, section III considers the use of legal authorities in both substantive and procedural disputes, comparing the responses of common law and civil law adjudicators with respect to each type of dispute as well as across the substantive-procedural divide and again testing longstanding theoretical assumptions against recently obtained empirical evidence. The analysis then moves in section IV to a discussion of how legal reasoning among both common law- and civil law-trained adjudicators might be improved through continuing professional education. The suggestions contained in this section are based not only on best practices in judicial and arbitral education but also on data gleaned from a recent empirical study of judges and arbitrators from around the world. Finally, the Article concludes in section V with a number of forward-looking observations.

Before beginning, it is useful to provide some basic information about the research methodology associated with the empirical data presented in this Article.[4] Appendices I through IV contain four charts derived from a large-scale, multi-pronged study recently conducted by the author of legal reasoning in commercial disputes.[5] The information found in the Appendices was generated from an anonymous online survey of 465 judges and arbitrators from around the world who were asked to discuss legal reasoning in national and international commercial disputes.[6]

Respondents included individuals from both the common law and civil law traditions.[7] The common law countries represented, calculated to the hundredth of a percentage point based on the total number of respondents indicating they were qualified in a common law jurisdiction (N=322), include Australia (0.62%), the Bahamas (0.31%), Canada (4.35%), Hong Kong (0.93%), India (0.62%), Singapore (0.31%), the United Kingdom (6.83%) and the United States (86.02%). The civil law countries represented, calculated to the hundredth of a percentage point based on the total number of respondents indicating they were qualified in a civil law jurisdiction (N=83), include Argentina (2.41%), Austria (2.41%), Belarus (2.41%), Belgium (7.23%), Bolivia (1.20%), Brazil (7.23%), Colombia (2.41%), Denmark (1.20%), Egypt (1.20%), Finland (1.20%), France (13.25%), Germany (9.64%), Greece (1.20%), Guatemala (1.20%), Italy (4.82%), Latvia (1.20%), Mexico (3.61%), the Netherlands (1.20%), Norway (1.20%), Paraguay (1.20%), Peru (1.20%), Spain (8.43%), Sweden (3.61%), Switzerland (14.46%), Turkey (1.20%), Uzbekistan (1.20%), and Venezuela (2.41%).

Three of the four charts (Appendices I-III) involve questions where survey participants were asked to indicate the relative importance of various items, where five was considered "very important" and one was considered "not important at all".[8] The fourth chart (Appendix IV) involved a question where respondents were asked to indicate whether certain topics must be addressed (rated five out of five) or need not be addressed (rated one out of five). The charts separate common law from civil law responses and report the weighted average of responses relating to each entry, followed by the standard deviation in parenthesis, followed by the total number of responses relating to that particular item and concluding with the rank of that item within the cohort's responses for that question.

Potential differences between common law and civil law responses were analysed by considering: (1) the relative standing of the various responses to each question within each cohort (i.e. common law respondents or civil law respondents), (2) the relative standing of the responses to each question between the two cohorts and (3) the statistical significance of the difference between intensity markings of the two cohorts with respect to individual responses. The cross-group intensity comparisons were reported in a separate column and relied on a t-statistical test, which compares the mean of two independent populations ($\mu 1$ and $\mu 2$) along a single variable to determine whether any difference exists other than that attributable to chance. Statistical significance was deemed to exist in cases with an alpha (a1) level of $p<.05$ or lower.[9] The study reports p levels of .05 (designated by a single asterisk), .01 (designated by two asterisks) and .001 (designated by three asterisks).[10]

While the study provides a number of very interesting insights into common law and civil law perspectives on legal reasoning, it does not focus solely on disputes arising in international commercial arbitration. As noted previously, the study included both judges and arbitrators, and allowed participants to discuss commercial disputes that were both domestic and international in nature.[11] Although the number of respondents who identified solely as judges was dwarfed by the number of individuals who had acted as arbitrators, either exclusively or in addition to acting as a judge, the text will refer to both judicial decisions and arbitral awards (jointly characterised as "reasoned rulings") except when the two can and should be distinguished.[12] Notably, the inclusion of judges and domestic arbitrators in this study is by no means problematic to the current analysis, since the goal of the Article is to identify whether and to what extent any differences in legal reasoning arise across the common law-civil law divide. Indeed, inclusion of judges and domestic arbitrators may give a more realistic view of standard practices in common law and civil law jurisdictions, since those individuals are less likely to reflect the type of "transnationalised" mindset that some commentators believe exists in international commercial arbitration.[13]

II. REASONED RULINGS: DEFINITIONS, DISTINCTIONS AND MOTIVATIONS

II.A. Theoretical Considerations

II.A.1. Defining reasoned rulings

The first matter to consider involves the question of what constitutes a fully reasoned judicial decision or arbitral award in international commercial disputes. In cross-border litigation, the matter is determined by national practice, as outlined in the relevant rules of civil and judicial procedure, while in arbitration, the matter is typically defined by institutional rules. However, in both settings, the governing provisions are often quite vague and simply indicate that an award should include "reasons", with little if any explanation as to what is entailed by that term.[14]

To some extent, the absence of detail regarding the shape and content of a reasoned ruling may be the result of the difficulties inherent in describing what constitutes adequate legal reasoning as an abstract proposition. Indeed, it is often easier to identify specific examples of fully reasoned decisions and awards than it is to provide a categorical definition of what constitutes adequate legal reasoning.[15]

Some assistance may be gained from the world of investment arbitration, where Tai-Heng Cheng and Robert Trisotto have argued that the reasoning requirement reflected in institutional rule sets

> is in fact a reasoning standard. Disagreements among [annulment] committees about whether the standard should be high or low are... fundamentally about what methods of reasoning are acceptable. The high standard countenances only reasoning that is correct on the law and facts and the rational derivation of outcomes therefrom; the low standard tolerates reasoning that is incorrect due to mistakes in the law or facts, so long as the reasoning is internally consistent; and the intermediate standard requires coherence and permits errors of law and fact, so long as these errors are reasonable errors.[16]

Similar types of studies have not yet been conducted in international commercial arbitration, likely because of the difficulties associated with obtaining original awards in their entirety. However, Gary Born has noted that being correct as a matter of law (i.e. the high standard identified by Cheng and Trisotto in the investment context) is "not a requirement for a well-reasoned [commercial] award: bad or unpersuasive reasons are still reasons, and satisfy statutory requirements for reasoned awards."[17]

Additional guidance may be obtained from domestic sources. For example, the State of Pennsylvania has described a reasoned ruling in an administrative law dispute in the following terms:

> [A]ll findings of fact shall be based upon sufficient competent evidence to justify same. All parties to an adjudicatory proceeding are entitled to a reasoned decision containing findings of fact and conclusions of law based upon the evidence as a whole which clearly and concisely states and explains the rationale for the decisions so that all can determine why and how a particular result was reached. The... judge shall specify the evidence upon which the... judge relies and state the reasons for accepting it in conformity with this section. When faced with conflicting evidence, the... judge must adequately explain the reasons for rejecting or discrediting competent evidence. Uncontroverted evidence may not be rejected for no reason or for an irrational reason; the... judge must identify that evidence and explain adequately the reasons for its rejection.[18]

As useful as this definition is, it may still fall somewhat short in practice, since finding "the appropriate methodology for distinguishing questions of fact from questions of law [is], to say the least, elusive."[19] Indeed, "the practical truth [is] that the decision to label an issue a 'question of law', a 'question of fact', or a 'mixed question of law and fact' is sometimes as much a matter of allocation as it is of analysis."[20]

Although reasoned rulings have long played a central role in the common law legal tradition, civil law jurisdictions also consider fully reasoned legal decisions to be essential to procedural justice.[21] However, a reasoned decision in a civil law nation can not only look very different from a reasoned decision in a common law country, it can also vary significantly in comparison to other civil law decisions.[22] At one end of the spectrum lie French judgments, which are usually "formulated in a single sentence, including several 'whereas-es' (*attendus*)".[23] Although some common law commentators appear to believe that "French practice belies the notion that well-reasoned [apparently meaning fully reasoned] opinions are in some sense necessary",[24] French decisions have been described as being "consistent with—and probably produced by—the primacy of text, conceptualism, and deduction, as well as the post-revolutionary caution on the part of judges not to exceed their limited powers."[25]

As well-known as the French style may be, it is by no means standard within the civil law legal tradition. For example, it has been said that

> [w]hoever compares the arguments of a decision of a German Landgericht with those of a Dutch rechtbank will be impressed by the length and thoroughness of the German argument on the one hand, the straightforward, paper-saving decision of the Dutch court on the other. In appeal courts and before the highest courts the differences in elaborateness are even more apparent. German legal style is much more differentiated, scholarly worded; the style of Dutch courts is pragmatic....[26]

Furthermore, the French approach does not appear to have been routinely adopted in international commercial arbitration, despite the esteem with which France is held in the field.[27] Instead, reasoned awards in international commercial arbitration more frequently resemble judicial decisions generated by courts in common law countries and in civil law jurisdictions like Germany.[28]

The difficulties associated with defining reasoned rulings both within and between different legal systems suggest that further analysis should proceed on a functional basis.[29] This approach is particularly useful because it not only overcomes differences between litigation and arbitration but also between common law and civil law traditions.[30] The discussion will therefore move to considering structural and non-structural rationales for reasoned rulings.

II.A.2. Structural rationales for reasoned rulings

Perhaps the most well-known structural rationale for reasoned rulings involves the common law concept of *stare decisis*, which requires judges to adhere to legal principles established in judgments rendered by courts whose decisions are binding upon the ruling court.[31] Because *stare decisis* does not technically apply in civil law jurisdictions or in international commercial arbitration, this rationale may not initially appear relevant outside common law courts.[32] However, judges in a number of civil law countries routinely follow the decisions of higher level courts, even if the principle of precedent is not part of that particular legal system, so as to promote predictability and consistency in the law.[33] Arbitral awards can also generate a type of persuasive authority, particularly matters involving arbitral procedure, again as a result of the need for predictability and consistency.[34] Thus, reasoned awards and civil law decisions may be said to meet this first type of structural purpose, even if *stare decisis* does not technically apply outside of common law courts.

Reasoned rulings serve other structural purposes. For example, courts in both common law and civil law countries use reasoned rulings to give context to lower court decisions and thereby help appellate courts determine whether and to what extent the judgment below should be upheld.[35] This rationale might also initially appear inapplicable to international commercial arbitration, since most jurisdictions do not allow courts to review the merits of an arbitral award.[36] However, some jurisdictions, most notably England, allow judicial appeals of international awards, which could be seen as providing arbitrators with a strong incentive to render fully reasoned awards in arbitrations seated in England.[37]

Although arbitral awards are seldom reviewed on the merits, they may be subject to other types of post-award scrutiny. The most likely of these types of actions involve efforts to vacate or enforce an arbitral award, domestically or internationally.[38] Although these actions typically focus on procedural concerns, the likelihood of a challenge being brought in the first place may be affected by the quality of the reasoning found in the underlying award.[39] For example, a well-written, fully reasoned award may persuade the losing party that a decision is well-supported, even if the outcome is negative.[40] Alternatively, a fully reasoned award may diminish the likelihood of a judicial challenge by eliminating certain grounds for non-enforcement.[41]

Another possible action involves collateral or parallel proceedings.[42] Although the law concerning preclusion and collateral estoppel are not as well developed in arbitration as in litigation,[43] a court or arbitral tribunal may find itself unable to give preclusive effect to an award that is not fully reasoned, since such an award may not indicate whether a particular issue was fully and fairly addressed in the earlier proceeding.[44]

The final type of post-award procedure to consider involves arbitral appeals. Over the last few years, several arbitral organisations have adopted special rule sets governing appellate arbitration.[45] Arbitral appeals have important ramifications for the award writing process, both at first instance and on appeal.[46] For example, arbitrators hearing a dispute as an initial matter may need to be increasingly aware of the quality of their awards both to avoid creating an appealable issue[47] and to provide an appellate tribunal with a solid understanding of how and why the initial decision was made.[48]

II.A.3. Non-structural rationales for reasoned rulings

Although lawyers are generally familiar with structural rationales for reasoned rulings, various non-structural rationales also exist. First, reasoned rulings have been said to constitute part of a "procedural trinity that is necessary to establish the rule of law", although the strength and nature of this element may vary somewhat across the common law-civil law divide.[49] For example, Mathilde Cohen has observed that,

> [i]n the common law tradition, judicial reason-giving does not attach to individual right holders. Litigants or defendants have no enforceable right to reasoned decisions; a judge's failure to give reasons does not amount to reversible error. The validity of the judgment is evaluated independently from the reasons given for it. Unreasoned decisions are protected by the

> "harmless error" doctrine. The rationale behind this rule appears to be judicial economy. No appeal lies on the grounds that a court gave inadequate or insufficient reasons. A successful appeal must contend that the judgment was incorrect and thus warrants reversal.[50]

In contrast, some civil law jurisdictions consider the absence of reasons to be "a procedural defect that warrants voiding the judgment altogether."[51]

Arbitration also respects and protects procedural fairness, with Catherine Rogers recognising that "the product of international arbitral decision-making is justice".[52] While some jurisdictions allow parties in arbitration to waive the right to a reasoned award, other countries do not.[53] Furthermore, even when a waiver is allowed, parties in international commercial disputes seldom take advantage of that opportunity.[54] Thus, while the reasoning requirement in international commercial arbitration may differ from similar standards applicable in litigation,[55] it is clear that arbitrators must provide some minimal level of reasoning once the parties have requested a reasoned award.[56] As it turns out, the length and details commonly associated with reasoned awards in international commercial arbitration suggest that many arbitral tribunals are far exceeding any minimum requirements.[57]

Second, reasoned rulings are believed to improve the quality of the decision-making process and consequently of the decision or award itself.[58] As U.S. Circuit Judge Richard Posner once said, "[r]easoning that seemed sound when 'in the head' may seem half-baked when written down, especially since the written form of an argument encourages some degree of critical detachment in the writer, who in reading what he [or she] has written will be wondering how an audience would react."[59] By forcing judges and arbitrators to articulate their thought processes, reasoned rulings help "rationalize the... process", "safeguard against arbitrary decisions", "prevent consideration of improper and irrelevant factors", "minimize the risk of reliance upon inaccurate information", and "attain[...] institutional objective[s] of dispensing equal and impartial justice" while simultaneously "demonstrat[ing] to society that these goals are being met".[60]

Third, reasoned rulings can enhance the legitimacy of the dispute resolution process, either in general or with respect to the immediate proceeding, by demonstrating the integrity of the judicial or arbitral endeavour.[61] This factor may be of particular relevance to international arbitration, which has come under increasing attack in recent years, with critics indicating concerns about the lack of transparency and the supposedly preferential treatment of large, multinational firms.[62] Fully reasoned arbitral awards can help assuage fears about the quality of justice provided by arbitrators by detailing the high degree of care and knowledge that go into the decision-making process.

Fourth and finally, reasoned awards provide parties with a more robust explanation of why the arbitral tribunal decided as it did.[63] This feature can be quite important, since empirical studies have shown that "the perceived fairness of arbitration hearings significantly predicts litigant decisions to accept an arbitration decision",[64] which suggests that parties who believe that they have not been fully "heard" during the arbitration, as reflected by the quality or content of the reasoning enunciated in the written award, might be more inclined to mount a challenge to that award.[65]

II.B. Empirical Findings

Having set forth the theoretical reasons for reasoned awards, the next step involves testing those assumptions against empirical observations. Appendix I contains responses to a survey question asking judges and arbitrators from both common law and civil law countries to identify factors used to determine how detailed a reasoned decision or award should be.[66] The question was framed in this way to avoid confusion among the respondents about whether a reasoned ruling should be written in the first place, since that matter is often controlled by external factors, particularly in arbitration, where arbitration agreements or arbitral rules frequently mandate the type of award that is to be rendered.[67] While judges may be able to exercise slightly more discretion as to whether they will write a fully reasoned decision, external influences may nevertheless exist in the form of pressure from chief judges and/or the court's internal norms of judicial procedure.[68]

The question focused on nine different alternatives drawn from the theoretical literature on legal reasoning and asked respondents to indicate how important each item was, based on a five-point scale, where one was the least important and five was the most important. The resulting data was analysed with respect to (1) the relative standing of the nine options within each cohort (i.e. common law respondents or civil law respondents), (2) the relative standing of the nine options between the two cohorts and (3) the statistical significance of the difference between intensity markings of the two cohorts.

As Appendix I shows, the responses to this question were remarkably similar across the common law-civil law divide. Not only were the first five responses identical as between common law and civil law participants, but the intensity of the first five responses showed no statistically significant difference between the two groups. This information is useful in offsetting the common assumption that structural considerations (such as those relating to the need to create and establish common law precedent) are the most important motivations for reasoned rulings.

This conclusion is further supported by the nature of the top five responses. For example, the most highly ranked responses focused on content-based considerations, with the number-one answer citing the difficulty, complexity or novelty of the dispute as a matter of fact (rather than of law) and the number-two answer, by a very small margin of intensity, citing the difficult, complexity or novelty of the dispute as a matter of law (rather than of fact). While this information does not address the question of whether respondents engaged in deductive versus inductive reasoning, a concept that has long been believed to differentiate common law versus civil law reasoning,[69] the data nevertheless suggest that judges and lawyers approach the writing process similarly across the common law-civil law divide.

The third most common response in both groups indicated that the act of writing helped the respondent think through the materials, thereby increasing the likelihood of reaching the right outcome. While common law lawyers rated this item slightly higher in absolute terms, giving it a 4.21 out of 5.00 as opposed to civil law lawyers' 3.90, the difference was not statistically significant. What is intriguing, however, is the acknowledgement that the act of writing helps the analytical process, something that had been posited as a theoretical matter.[70]

The fourth most common response indicated that judges and arbitrators believe it is important to make sure that the losing party feels heard, something that has also been said to be important by theoretical commentators.[71] Interestingly, survey respondents also indicated that it was important to make sure that the winning party felt heard but at a much lower level of intensity, with that option appearing as the eighth highest-ranking alternative out of nine among both common law and civil law respondents.

The fifth most important factor involved the desire to increase the perceived legitimacy of the particular award at issue, a concept that is related to commentators' observations about the connection between reasoned rulings and legitimacy.[72] Although the intensity of this choice varied slightly between the two groups, earning a 3.92 out of 5.00 from common law lawyers and only a 3.67 from civil law lawyers, the difference was not statistically significant.

At this point, the hierarchical rankings began to diverge. Only two demonstrated statistically significant differences ($p<.05$) between common law and civil law respondents. One involved concerns about whether the losing party would challenge the resulting decision or award, with civil law lawyers giving this item intensity marks of 3.60 out of 5.00 and ranking it as the sixth most important factor to their determination of how detailed a reasoned ruling should be, while common law lawyers gave this factor a mark of 3.03 and ranked it as the least most important factor (ninth out of nine) to the question of how detailed a reasoned ruling should be. The other area of divergence involved the desire to increase the perceived legitimacy of the dispute resolution process in question (i.e. arbitration or litigation as a general proposition), as opposed to the legitimacy of the particular decision or award at issue. Common law lawyers ranked this as the seventh most important factor to the question of how detailed a reasoned ruling should be and gave it an intensity marking of 3.34 out of 5.00, while civil law lawyers ranked this factor as ninth out of nine, with an intensity ranking of 2.90.

Interestingly, both common law and civil law lawyers considered the nature of the legal dispute in question (i.e. the type of substantive claims at issue) to be relatively unimportant to the determination of how detailed a reasoned decision or award should be. Common law lawyers ranked this option as their sixth most important factor, with an intensity mark of 3.68 out of 5.00, and civil law lawyers ranked it as their seventh most important factor, with an intensity mark of 3.57. However, the difference in intensity ratings was not statistically significant.

The data generated by this question is useful in that it confirms a number of theoretical assumptions about the motivations behind reasoned rulings and demonstrates a high degree of consistency across the common law-civil law divide. However, it is possible to gain even more information about the nature of the reasoning process itself, as discussed in the next subsection.

III. USE OF LEGAL AUTHORITIES IN SUBSTANTIVE AND PROCEDURAL DISPUTES

III.A. Theoretical Considerations

The next item to consider involves the use of legal authorities by common law- and civil law-trained individuals when resolving substantive and procedural disputes. Although a number of assumptions exist about the differences between common law and civil law reasoning,[73] one of the most frequently mentioned involves claims about the types of legal authority that are considered most persuasive in particular jurisdictions. For example, conventional wisdom suggests that common law lawyers find judicial decisions to be the most important type of legal authority while civil law lawyers are said to downplay the importance of such materials.[74] Conversely, commentators frequently claim that civil law lawyers have a heightened regard for scholarly commentary as compared to the relatively minimal role that scholarship plays in common law jurisdictions.[75]

Although most comparative analyses relating to the use and priority of legal authorities in common law and civil law jurisdictions focus on questions of substantive law,[76] some comparative procedural analyses exist courtesy of international commercial arbitration.[77] These latter studies distinguish between seven types of legal authority: (1) international conventions and treaties; (2) national arbitration laws; (3) arbitral rules, such as those published by arbitral institutions, and other forms of arbitral soft law; (4) the law of the dispute, which can include agreements between the parties, procedural orders issued by the arbitral tribunal and previously rendered arbitral awards involving the parties; (5) arbitral awards not involving the parties to the immediate dispute, meaning awards that have been published in whole or in part in arbitral reporters or as made public as exhibits to judicial proceedings; (6) judicial decisions; and (7) scholarly commentary.[78] This list is useful because it recognises the importance of both public and private sources of law and therefore formed the basis for survey questions regarding the use of legal authorities in substantive and procedural disputes.

III.B. Empirical Findings

Over the last few decades, questions have arisen about longstanding theoretical assumptions about the relative weight of different legal authorities in common law and civil law legal systems.[79] Not only have some commentators suggested that statutes are now nearly as important in common law countries as they are in civil law countries, but some civil law jurisdictions are said to rely on judicial decisions in much the same way that common law jurisdictions do.[80] As intriguing as these hypotheses are, they have not been supported by rigorous empirical research.[81] However, that situation has changed as a result of recent studies on legal reasoning in commercial disputes.[82] Not only does this new empirical work consider potential differences between the use of legal authorities in common law and civil law countries in both substantive and procedural disputes, it also evaluates potential differences across the substantive-procedural divide.

The data is reproduced in Appendices II and III. The analysis begins with Appendix II, which considers the importance of ten different types of legal authorities associated with the determination of substantive disputes. In some ways, the survey findings confirm the standard theoretical understanding of how legal authorities are used and weighed in common law and civil law jurisdictions. For example, the five most important authorities for common law judges and arbitrators were, in decreasing order of importance: (1) judicial decisions from the jurisdiction whose law controls the issue; (2) domestic regulations, statutes or administrative rules; (3) judicial decisions from jurisdictions other than the jurisdiction whose law controls the matter; (4) legislative histories of domestic regulations, statutes or administrative rules; and (5) scholarly works. However, judges and arbitrators from the civil law tradition indicated that the five most important authorities for determining substantive disputes were, in decreasing order of importance: (1) domestic regulations, statutes or administrative rules; (2) international treaties; (3) judicial decisions from the jurisdiction whose law controls the matter; (4) scholarly works; and (5) soft law. While the relatively high status of international treaties could be attributed to the fact that a relatively high proportion of civil law respondents indicated that they were focusing on international rather than domestic disputes,[83] it is also consistent with the fact that most civil law nations adopt a monist perspective to international law.[84]

As useful as the hierarchical data is in comparing how common law and civil law lawyers conduct legal reasoning in substantive disputes, the intensity marks are equally illuminating. Seven of the ten types of legal authority showed a statistically significant difference between the two cohorts. Five items reflected differences at the highest level of statistical significance ($p<.001$): international treaties, which featured an intensity mark of 2.62 out of 5.00 from common law respondents and an intensity mark of 4.37 from civil law respondents; judicial decisions from the jurisdiction whose law controls the matter, which featured intensity marks of 4.76 from common law respondents and 4.35 from civil law respondents; judicial decisions from jurisdictions other than the jurisdiction whose law controls the matter, which were given intensity marks of 3.19 by common law respondents and 2.39 by civil law respondents; legislative history of international treaties (travaux préparatoires), which earned intensity marks of 2.00 from common law respondents and 3.00 from civil law respondents; and scholarly works, which won intensity marks of 2.91 from common law respondents and 3.54 from civil law respondents. Two type of authorities—arbitral awards involving parties other than those involved in the instant dispute and soft law—reflected a statistically significant degree of difference between common law and civil law respondents at an intermediate level of confidence ($p<.01$).[85] These results, like those generated from the hierarchical rankings, confirm the standard understanding of how common law and civil law training affects legal reasoning in substantive disputes.

However, the inquiry did not stop there. Instead, the survey also asked judges and arbitrators to identify the importance of different types of legal authorities when deciding procedural disputes, offering the same list of ten authorities that were discussed with respect to substantive disputes. Interestingly, survey respondents did not place the authorities in the same hierarchical order that was seen with substantive disputes, nor did the respondents give the individual alternatives the same intensity ratings.

As Appendix III shows, common law and civil law respondents showed a much higher level of convergence with respect to the relative importance of procedural authorities as compared to substantive authorities. First, the two cohorts agreed on the two most important types of procedural authority: (1) judicial decisions from the jurisdiction whose law controls the matter and (2) domestic regulations, states or administrative rules which, in the procedural context, would mean rules of civil procedure (in litigation) and national laws on arbitration (in arbitration). Second, the two groups came to very similar conclusions about the importance of scholarly works, with common law respondents putting that particular authority in a tie for third place along with arbitral awards involving the parties to the instant dispute and civil law respondents placing scholarly works in fourth position. The remaining authorities reflected varying levels of divergence between the different types of authority.

Useful information was also generated with respect to intensity rankings. For example, the intensity marks for the first two categories of legal authorities (i.e. those on which the respondents were in agreement as to relative importance) did not differ to a statistically significant degree, even though six of the remaining eight items did. Four of those additional authorities—international treaties, legislative history of international treaties, scholarly works and soft law—differed at the highest level of confidence ($p<.001$), while two authorities—arbitral awards involving parties other than those involved in the immediate dispute and judicial decisions from jurisdictions other than the jurisdiction whose law controls the matter—differed at an intermediate level of confidence ($p<.01$).

As useful as it is to analyse Appendix II and Appendix III independently, comparing the two charts yields a number of unique insights not reflected in any other known studies. First, the data suggests that traditional views about how common law- and civil law-trained lawyers view legal authorities may be incorrect when it comes to procedural authorities. For example, respondents from the civil law rated judicial decisions more highly in procedural disputes than in substantive disputes, thereby resembling common law lawyers, while respondents from the common law rated scholarly works more highly in procedural disputes than in substantive disputes, thereby resembling civil law lawyers. While it remains unclear at this point why judges and arbitrators approach substantive and procedural disputes differently, this finding opens the door to additional research.[86]

Second, those from civil law countries appear to be more consistent than those from common law countries with respect to their approach to legal authorities across the substantive-procedural divide. For example, civil law respondents placed the same authorities in the top five positions in both types of disputes, with only a relatively minor rearrangement of individual items in terms of relative importance.[87] In contrast, common law respondents displayed a much greater degree of variation across the substantive-procedural divide in terms of how they rated their top five authorities.

Finally, Appendices II and III show that, for the most part, civil law respondents tended to rate substantive authorities at a slightly higher intensity rate than was the case with procedural authorities, although that difference may not be statistically significant.[88] The same phenomenon also appeared to be true with respect to the common law respondents, although such comparisons are more difficult since, as noted, common law lawyers perceived the relative importance of individual authorities in more varied terms as between substantive and procedural disputes.

As with most forms of empirical research, this data merely reports what judges and arbitrators believe with respect to the importance of various authorities. It does not confirm whether the reported beliefs are also reflected in action,[89] nor does it seek to establish why respondents believe what they do. However, the information gained from this study provides interesting avenues for future research on this issue.

IV. CONTINUING PROFESSIONAL EDUCATION ON LEGAL REASONING

IV.A. Theoretical Considerations

Although relatively few studies exist regarding the need for and nature of continuing professional education of judges and arbitrators, recent empirical research indicates that this is a field that deserves more attention. Indeed, according to the survey discussed elsewhere in this Article, 79 per cent of common law respondents and 68 per cent of civil law respondents believed that new and experienced judges and arbitrators would benefit from additional educational programming on writing reasoned decisions and awards.[90] This data is supported by scholarly and practical commentary suggesting that the skills associated with serving as a judge or arbitrator differ significantly from those associated with acting as an advocate, with new adjudicators often finding "the 'move from advocacy to decision, from marshalling and presenting evidence to fact-finding and synthesizing', to be extremely challenging."[91] As a result, it is "inaccurate to claim, as some authorities have, that international arbitrators can gain the necessary skillset simply through 'observation, exposure, participation and experience'."[92]

Although continuing education of judges and arbitrators appears to be considered increasingly important, questions exist as to what precisely should be taught. In the past, educational providers often followed the law school model of legal education, emphasizing content-based programming that discussed recent developments in substantive or procedural law or policy.[93] More recently, various for-profit and advocacy-oriented groups have offered judicial education courses on complex and often controversial subjects, raising concerns about the objectivity of the programming.[94] However, national and international leaders in judicial studies have begun to shift professional programming away from current events and private provider models and toward multidisciplinary curricula that include more diverse coursework, including what has been called "judge-craft".[95] This approach has been emulated to some degree in arbitral settings, with some providers offering instruction on how to write a reasoned decision or award, although most of those programmes appear to focus on relatively basic or mechanistic concerns.[96]

IV.B. Empirical Findings

As judicial and arbitral education becomes more sophisticated, it becomes increasingly important to understand what judges and arbitrators need and want in order to improve their performance as adjudicators. Appendix IV shows responses to a question asking judges and arbitrators to rate eleven different types of issues that might be included in continuing professional programming on a scale of one to five, where one indicated items that did not need to be addressed and five indicated items that must be addressed.

Interestingly, very few similarities existed across the common law-civil law divide. Indeed, the only item that was ranked the same for the two cohorts was the desire for programming on how to structure reasoned decisions or awards, which was the first choice for both groups.[97] However, a statistically significant degree of intensity existed ($p<.001$) with respect to this particular topic, with civil law respondents being more strongly in favour of programming on this particular point, rating it at 4.64 out of 5.00, as compared to the 4.25 mark from common law respondents. This difference may be due at least in part to the fact that a relative low number (19 per cent) of civil law-trained judges and arbitrators participating in the study in question had attended a seminar on writing reasoned decisions or awards in comparison to common law-trained judges and arbitrators (57 per cent), a difference that was statistically significant ($p<.001$).[98]

Immediately after this point, the data began to diverge. Civil law respondents rated the need to learn how to weigh different pieces of evidence as the second most important element, with common law respondents ranking that topic as only seventh out of eleven. The difference in intensity of interest in this subject was also statistically significant ($p<.001$), with civil law respondents giving this subject a mark of 4.08 out of 5.00 and common law respondents giving it only a 3.20.

The second most important topic for judges and arbitrators from common law countries involved how to apply the facts to the governing legal standard. This item was only fourth in importance to civil law respondents, although civil law respondents indicated a higher intensity of interest than common law respondents did, giving it a mark of 4.00 out of 5.00, as compared to 3.83 for common law respondents. However, the difference in intensity rankings was not statistically significant.

The third most highly rated topic for common law respondents—how other judges or arbitrators approach reasoned decisions or awards—was the tenth most important item for civil law respondents, although the difference in intensity ranking was not statistically important. The third most important item for civil law respondents—how to identify the governing legal standard—was the fifth most important factor to common law respondents, and the intensity ranking (4.03 out of 5.00 for civil law respondents and 3.39 for common law respondents) reflected a statistically significant difference ($p<.01$).

Notably, none of the respondents indicated that they wanted more information involving current developments in law or practice.[99] This suggests that providers of judicial and arbitral education would do well to shift their focus away from law-school type programming, where the content of the law is of primary importance, and toward a more skills-based curriculum consistent with contemporary best practices in the field of judicial studies.

V. CONCLUSION

International commercial arbitration has long been praised for transforming the once-arcane field of comparative law into "a kind of 'living comparison' of laws... emerging from the continuous communication between persons educated in different intellectual and legal contexts."[100] Indeed, international commercial arbitration has become one of the major "clients" of comparative law as arbitrators and advocates seek to improve their understanding of how foreign legal systems operate.[101] Unfortunately, most of the knowledge about the differences between common law and civil law legal systems appears to be somewhat outdated and based more on anecdote rather than evidence.

This Article has sought to counteract conventional wisdom by testing various longstanding assumptions about legal reasoning in common law and civil law countries against recent empirical research in that field. While much remains to be done,[102] this Article has nevertheless provided new and important insights into comparative commercial dispute resolution. In so doing, this Article hopes not only to provide parties and practitioners with useful data that will assist them in presenting their cases to judges and arbitrators, but also to help scholars develop new avenues of theoretical and empirical analysis.

APPENDIX I[103]

Factors important to the determination of how detailed a reasoned decision or award should be (weighted averages, followed by standard deviation in parenthesis, sample (N) size and ranking within the relevant cohort)

Statistical significance is indicated by asterisk, where one asterisk (*) indicates $p<.05$, two asterisks (**) indicate $p<.01$, and three asterisks (***) indicate $p<.001$

	Common law	**Civil law**	**Common law—Civil law t-statistic**
I believe the difficulty, complexity or novelty of the dispute as a matter of fact requires an in-depth explanation of my reasoning	4.32 (.88) 227 Rank: 1	4.26 (.90) 43 Rank: 1	-.41
I believe the difficulty, complexity or novelty of the dispute as a matter of law requires an in-depth explanation of my reasoning	4.31 (.91) 227 Rank: 2	4.17 (1.03) 42 Rank: 2	-.90
I believe the nature of the legal dispute (i.e., the type of substantive claims at issue) requires an in-depth explanation of my reasoning	3.68 (1.15) 226 Rank: 6	3.57 (1.13) 42 Rank: 7	-.57
I find the act of writing a reasoned decision or award helps me think through the analytical process and increases the likelihood of reaching the right outcome	4.21 (1.08) 225 Rank: 3	3.90 (1.12) 42 Rank: 3	-1.70
I want to increase the perceived legitimacy of this particular decision or award	3.92 (1.10) 224 Rank 5	3.67 (1.16) 42 Rank: 5	-1.34
I want to increase the perceived legitimacy of this type of dispute resolution process (i.e., litigation or arbitration)	3.34 (1.32) 226 Rank: 7	2.90 (1.23) 42 Rank: 9	-2.00*
I want to make sure the losing party feels heard	3.93 (1.04) 226 Rank: 4	3.76 (1.07) 41 Rank: 4	-.96
I want to make sure the winning party feels heard	3.32 (1.24) 225 Rank: 8	3.07 (1.13) 42 Rank: 8	-1.22
I want to minimize the likelihood the losing party will seek to challenge the decision or award	3.03 (1.39) 225 Rank: 9	3.60 (1.27) 42 Rank: 6	2.47*

APPENDIX II[104]

Importance of different types of legal authorities when deciding substantive disputes (weighted averages, followed by standard deviation in parenthesis, sample (N) size and ranking within the relevant cohort)

Statistical significance is indicated by asterisk, where one asterisk (*) indicates p<.05, two asterisks (**) indicate p<.01, and three asterisks (***) indicate p<.001.

	Common law	**Civil law**	**Common Law—Civil Law t-statistic**
Arbitral awards involving the parties to this dispute	2.79 (1.54) 261 Rank: 6	2.98 (1.42) 52 Rank: 7	1.24
Arbitral awards involving parties other than those involved in this dispute	1.75 (1.11) 262 Rank: 10	2.31 (.86) 54 Rank: 10	3.50**
Domestic regulations, statutes or administrative rules	4.41 (.92) 261 Rank: 2	4.46 (.84) 54 Rank: 1	.37
International treaties	2.62 (1.61) 255 Rank: 8	4.37 (.84) 52 Rank: 2	7.62***
Judicial decisions from the jurisdiction whose law controls the matter	4.76 (.52) 262 Rank: 1	4.35 (.78) 54 Rank: 3	-4.79***
Judicial decisions from jurisdictions other than the jurisdiction whose law controls the matter	3.19 (.89) 263 Rank: 3	2.39 (.83) 54 Rank: 9	-6.08***
Legislative history of domestic regulations, statutes or administrative rules	2.96 (1.07) 261 Rank: 4	2.96 (1.01) 54 Rank: 8	.00
Legislative history of int'l treaties (travaux préparatoires)	2.00 (1.15) 254 Rank: 9	3.00 (.89) 54 Rank: 6	6.02***
Scholarly works (articles, books, treatises)	2.91 (.98) 261 Rank: 5	3.54 (.75) 54 Rank: 4	4.46***
Soft law (i.e. non-binding but persuasive guidelines, declarations or codes of conduct)	2.70 (.86) 260 Rank: 7	3.09 (.96) 54 Rank: 5	2.97**

APPENDIX III[105]

Importance of different types of legal authorities when deciding procedural disputes (weighted averages, followed by standard deviation in parenthesis, sample (N) size and ranking within the relevant cohort)

Statistical significance is indicated by asterisk, where one asterisk (*) indicates $p<.05$, two asterisks (**) indicate $p<.01$, and three asterisks (***) indicate $p<.001$.

	Common law	Civil law	Common law—Civil law t-statistic
Arbitral awards involving the parties to this dispute	2.73 (1.53) 259 Rank: 3 (tied)	2.91 (1.43) 53 Rank: 6	.79
Arbitral awards involving parties other than those involved in this dispute	1.83 (1.09) 260 Rank: 9	2.26 (1.08) 53 Rank: 9	2.62**
Domestic regulations, statutes or administrative rules	3.78 (1.28) 261 Rank: 2	3.89 (1.34) 53 Rank: 2	.57
International treaties	2.17 (1.37) 252 Rank: 8	3.57 (1.31) 53 Rank: 3	6.81***
Judicial decisions from the jurisdiction whose law controls the matter	4.17 (1.13) 261 Rank: 1	3.94 (1.29) 53 Rank: 1	-1.32
Judicial decisions from jurisdictions other than the jurisdiction whose law controls the matter	2.68 (1.11) 260 Rank: 5	2.21 (.93) 53 Rank: 10	-2.88**
Legislative history of domestic regulations, statutes or administrative rules	2.53 (1.16) 258 Rank: 7	2.60 (1.13) 53 Rank: 7	.40
Legislative history of int'l treaties (travaux préparatoires)	1.75 (1.02) 252 Rank: 10	2.49 (.97) 53 Rank: 8	4.80***
Scholarly works (articles, books, treatises)	2.73 (1.02) 257 Rank: 3 (tied)	3.46 (.94) 52 Rank: 4	4.77***
Soft law (i.e. non-binding but persuasive guidelines, declarations or codes of conduct)	2.64 (1.01) 259 Rank: 6	3.23 (1.00) 52 Rank: 5	3.85***

APPENDIX IV[106]

Issues to be included in educational programming on reasoned decisions and awards (weighted averages, followed by standard deviation in parenthesis, sample (N) size and ranking within the relevant cohort)

Statistical significance is indicated by asterisk, where one asterisk (*) indicates p<.05, two asterisks (**) indicate p<.01, and three asterisks (***) indicate p<.001

	Common law	Civil law	Common law—Civil law t-statistic
How long and how detailed each section of a reasoned decision or award needs to be	2.87 (1.33) 196 Rank: 10	3.53 (1.25) 36 Rank: 9	2.76**
How long it takes judges or arbitrators to write a reasoned decision or award	2.37 (1.22) 199 Rank 11	2.64 (1.25) 36 Rank 11	1.22
How other judges or arbitrators approach reasoned decisions or awards	3.58 (1.10) 202 Rank: 3	3.47 (1.18) 36 Rank: 10	-.55
How to apply the facts to the governing legal standard	3.83 (1.17) 200 Rank: 2	4.00 (1.15) 36 Rank: 4	.80
How to approach substantive citation of legal materials (i.e., when to refer to legal authorities and how to analyse them in a reasoned decision or award, not what citation format to use)	3.38 (1.22) 200 Rank: 6	3.69 (.98) 36 Rank: 8	1.44
How to approach substantive citation of factual materials (i.e., when to refer to evidence and how to analyse evidence in a reasoned decision or award, not what citation format to use)	3.54 (1.18) 200 Rank: 4	3.94 (.98) 36 Rank: 5	1.92
How to distinguish material facts from immaterial facts	3.12 (1.33) 200 Rank: 9	3.77 (1.17) 35 Rank: 7	2.75**
How to identify the governing legal standard	3.39 (1.34) 200 Rank: 5	4.03 (1.16) 36 Rank: 3	2.69**
How to structure reasoned decisions or awards	4.25 (.92) 200 Rank: 1	4.64 (.64) 36 Rank: 1	2.44*
How to weigh different pieces of evidence	3.20 (1.26) 196 Rank: 7	4.08 (1.02) 36 Rank: 2	3.96***

	Common law	Civil law	Common law—Civil law t-statistic
How to weigh different legal authorities	3.17 (1.26) 196 Rank: 8	3.86 (1.05) 36 Rank: 6	3.09**

NOTES

1. S.I. Strong, *International Commercial Arbitration: A Guide for US Judges* (Federal Judicial Center 2012) 5-6, <http://www.fjc.gov> accessed 29 August 2019 (Strong, *Judicial Guide*) (comparing international commercial arbitration to transnational litigation).
2. *Rain CII Carbon, LLC* v *ConocoPhillips Co*, 674 F3d 469, 473-74 (5th Cir 2012) (distinguishing a standard award from a reasoned award); *Cat Charter, LLC v Schurtenberger*, 646 F3d 836, 844-46 (11th Cir 2011) (same); Gary B Born, *International Commercial Arbitration* (Wolters Kluwer 2014) 3037-45. The debate about what constitutes a reasoned award also arises in investment arbitration, although that subject is beyond the scope of the current Article. Tai-Heng Cheng and Robert Trisotto, "Reasons and Reasoning in Investment Treaty Arbitration", (2009) 32 *Suffolk Transnational Law Review* 409, 409; Jason Webb Yackee, "The Reasons Requirement in International Investment Arbitration: Critical Case Studies", (2009) 103 American Journal of International Law 629, 630.
3. These last two issues have recently been considered at length in a large-scale, multi-pronged empirical study. S.I. Strong, *Legal Reasoning Across Commercial Disputes: Comparing Judicial and Arbitral Analyses* (Oxford University Press forthcoming 2020) (Strong, *Legal Reasoning*) (considering legal reasoning in commercial disputes across the judicial-arbitral, national-international and common law-civil law divides).
4. For more on the methodology used in this survey, see ibid ch 3.
5. The full study includes several different research elements (a survey, a series of semi-structured interviews and a coded analysis of judicial decisions and arbitral awards) and is available elsewhere. ibid ch 1.
6. The full survey contained 37 different questions. ibid ch 3.
7. The survey also included respondents from other jurisdictions, but that data is not presented here, although it is discussed in the larger study. ibid.
8. The survey also allowed respondents to identify additional authorities by making "other" and providing a written-in response, but those responses are not discussed here in detail for reasons of space. For that data, see ibid figs. 3.5, 3.6, 3.35, 3.41.
9. Statistical significance refers to "the likelihood, or probability, that a statistic derived from a sample represents some genuine phenomenon in the population". Timothy C Urdan, *Statistics in Plain English (Routledge 2005) 50 (discussing statistical analysis in empirical legal research*); see also Lee Epstein and Gary King, "The Rules of Inference", (2002) 51 *University of Chicago Law Review* 1, 60; W Mark C Weidemaier, "Judging-Lite: How Arbitrators Use and Create Precedent", (2012) 90 *North Carolina Law Review* 1091, 1091.
10. T-statistics were calculated via Medcalc. Medcalc <https://www.medcalc.org/calc/comparison_of_means.php> accessed 29 August 2019. A *p* value of .05 means there is a 5 per cent likelihood (or less) that the difference between the two populations is attributable to chance, while a *p* level of .01 means there is a 1 per cent likelihood that the difference between the two populations is attributable to chance. *P* levels of .001 are even more robust, meaning that there is a .1 per cent likelihood that the difference between the two populations is random.
11. Distinctions between judicial and arbitral practice and between domestic and international practice can be found elsewhere. Strong, *Legal Reasoning* (n 3); S.I. Strong, "Legal Authorities and Comparative Law in International Commercial Arbitration: Best Practices Versus Empirically Determined Actual Practices", (forthcoming 2020) 1 *Ius Comparatum*.
12. Strong, *Legal Reasoning* (n 3) ch 3 (noting only 2 per cent of the 465 respondents indicated that they were acting only as judges, although a number of respondents had acted as both a judge and an arbitrator at some point in their careers). In many ways, judicial decisions are quite similar to reasoned awards in international commercial arbitration, at least at a structural level. Eg, ibid ch 5 (conducting a quantitative analysis comparing judicial decisions with national and international arbitral awards); S.I. Strong, "Reasoned Awards in International Commercial Arbitration: Embracing and Exceeding the Common Law-Civil Law Dichotomy", (2015) 37

Michigan Journal of International Law 1, 39-54 (Strong, Reasoned Awards); S.I. Strong, "Writing Reasoned Decisions and Opinions: A Guide for Novice, Experienced and Foreign Judges", 2015 Journal of Dispute Resolution 93, 117-27 (Strong, Reasoned Decisions).

13. Gabrielle Kaufmann-Kohler, "Arbitral Precedent: Dream, Necessity or Excuse?" (2007) 23 *Arbitration International* 357, 364 (noting "arbitrators have an inclination to 'transnationalize' the rules they apply"). Notably, this view is not universally held. Helena Whalen-Bridge, "The Reluctant Comparativist: Teaching Common Law Reasoning to Civil Law Students and the Future of Comparative Legal Skills", (2008) 58 *Journal of Legal Education* 364, 365 (noting the difficulty of setting aside one's initial legal training).

14. Mathilde Cohen, "When Judges Have Reasons Not to Give Reasons: A Comparative Law Approach", (2015) 72 *Washington and Lee Law Review* 483, 533 n286 (noting in some countries, the failure to give reasons provides grounds for overturning the judgment); Arizona Statute s 41-1092.08(A) ("The written decision shall contain a concise explanation of the reasons supporting the decision, including the findings of fact and conclusions of law."); International Centre for Dispute Resolution (ICDR) International Arbitration Rules, art 30(1) ("The tribunal shall state the reasons upon which the award is based, unless the parties have agreed that no reasons need be given."), <https://www.adr.org/Rules> accessed 29 August 2019; International Chamber of Commerce (ICC) Arbitration Rules, art 32(2) ("The award shall state the reasons upon which it is based."), <https://iccwbo.org/dispute-resolution-services/arbitration/rules-of-arbitration/> accessed 29 August 2019; London Court of International Arbitration (LCIA) Arbitration Rules, art 26.2 ("The Arbitral Tribunal shall make any award in writing and, unless all parties agree in writing otherwise, shall state the reasons upon which such award is based."), <https://www.lcia.org/Dispute_Resolution_Services/lcia-arbitration-rules-2014.aspx> accessed 29 August 2019; Stockholm Chamber of Commerce (SCC) Arbitration Rules, art 42(1) ("The Arbitral Tribunal shall make its award in writing, and, unless otherwise agreed by the parties, shall state the reasons upon which the award is based."), <https://sccinstitute.com/our-services/rules/> accessed 29 August 2019; United Nations Commission on International Trade Law (UNCITRAL) Arbitration Rules, art 34(3), GA Res 65/22, UN Doc A/RES/65/22 (Jan. 10, 2011) ("The arbitral tribunal shall state the reasons upon which the award is based, unless the parties have agreed that no reasons are to be given."). However, in practice, many standard procedural orders used by arbitrators contain phrases such as "The award shall contain the reasoning of the Arbitrator, applicable precedent and findings of fact and conclusions of law".

Although the Chinese International Economic and Trade Commission (CIETAC) adopts an approach similar to that of other arbitral institutions, CIETAC's language is a bit more fulsome and indicates that

> The arbitral tribunal shall state in the award the claims, the facts of the dispute, the reasons on which the award is based, the result of the award, the allocation of the arbitration costs, and the date on which and the place at which the award is made. The facts of the dispute and the reasons on which the award is based may not be stated in the award if the parties have so agreed, or if the award is made in accordance with the terms of a settlement agreement between the parties.

CIETAC Arbitration Rules, art 49(3), <http://www.cietac.org/index.php?m=Page&a=index&id=106&l=en> accessed 8 August 2019. Other relevant portions of the CIETAC rules state that

> 1. The arbitral tribunal shall independently and impartially render a fair and reasonable arbitral award based on the facts of the case and the terms of the contract, in accordance with the law, and with reference to international practices.
>
> ...
>
> 5. Where a case is examined by an arbitral tribunal composed of three arbitrators, the award shall be rendered by all three arbitrators or a majority of the arbitrators. A written dissenting opinion shall be kept with the file and may be appended to the award. Such dissenting opinion shall not form a part of the award.
> 6. Where the arbitral tribunal cannot reach a majority opinion, the arbitral award shall be rendered in accordance with the presiding arbitrator's opinion. The written opinions of the other arbitrators shall be kept with the file and may be appended to the award. Such written opinions shall not form a part of the award.
>
> ...
>
> ibid art 49.

15. *Hart v Massanari*, 266 F3d 1155, 1176-77 (9th Cir 2001) (discussing and reflecting the qualities of a reasoned ruling); The Green Bag Almanac and Reader, Exemplary Legal Writing, <http://www.greenbag.org/green_bag_press/almanacs/almanacs.html> accessed 29 August 2019 (listing well-written judicial rulings on an annual basis).

16. Cheng and Trisotto (n 2) 424.
17. Born (n 2) 3044.
18. 77 Pennsylvania Statutes Annotated s 834. Although this definition arises in the context of the statutory duties of a workers' compensation board, the principles appear to apply equally in other situations, including arbitration. Jennifer Kirby, "What Is An Award, Anyway?" (2014) 31 *Journal of International Arbitration* 475, 476; see also Born (n 2) 3040-41, 3043-44.
19. *Miller v Fenton*, 474 US 104, 113-14 (1985) (citations omitted).
20. ibid (citation omitted).
21. Cohen (n 14) 533; Michael L Wells, "'Sociological Legitimacy' in Supreme Court Opinion", (2007) 64 *Washington and Lee Law Review* 1011, 1029.
22. Marcel Fontaine, "Drafting the Award: A Perspective From a Civil Law Jurist", (1994) 5 ICC Court Bulletin 30, 33; Allen Shoenberger, "Change in the European Civil Law Systems: Infiltration of the Anglo-American Case Law System of Precedent Into the Civil Law System", (2009) 55 *Loyola Law Review* 5, 5.
23. Jeffrey L Friesen, "When Common Law Courts Interpret Civil Codes", (1996) 15 *Wisconsin International Law Journal* 1, 8; see also Louis Goutal, "Characteristics of Judicial Style in France, Britain and the USA", (1976) 24 *American Journal of Comparative Law* 43, 45.
24. Wells (n 21) 1029.
25. Friesen (n 23) 8.
26. Kai Schadbach, "The Benefits of Comparative Law: A Continental European View", (1998) 16 *Boston University International Law Journal* 331, 343 n63 (citing Erhard Blankenburg, "Patterns of Legal Culture: The Netherlands Compared to Neighboring Germany", (1998) 46 *American Journal of Comparative Law* 1, 40, and Arthur Taylor von Mehren and James Russell Gordley, *The Civil Law System, An Introduction to the Comparative Study of Law* (Little, Brown and Co 2d ed. 1977) 1140); Goutal (n 23) 45).
27. James M Gaitis, "International and Domestic Arbitration Procedure: The Need for a Rule Providing a Limited Opportunity for Arbitral Reconsideration of Reasoned Awards", (2004) 15 *American Review of International Arbitration* 9, 17 (describing what is typically included in a reasoned award); Fontaine (n 22) 36.
28. Fontaine (n 22) 36 (noting that French-style "whereas" clauses (*attendus*) are generally not used in international awards, even in those countries where that style of writing is common in the judicial context). But see Interim Award in ICC Case No 4131, IX *Yearbook Commercial Arbitration* 131, 135 (1984) (using *attendu* clauses, although the decision was translated from French and comes from an earlier era in international commercial arbitration). Indeed, most awards in international commercial arbitration run dozens of pages in length. e.g, *Contractor* (Zambia) *v Producer* (Zambia), Final Award, ICC Case No 16484, 2011, XXXIX *Yearbook Commercial Arbitration* 216 (2014); Fontaine (n 22) 36; Strong, *Legal Reasoning* (n 3) ch 5 (breaking down commercial awards on a paragraph-by-paragraph basis); see also XXXIX *Yearbook Commercial Arbitration* 30-305 (2014) (publishing a variety of recent awards); Schadbach (n 26) 343 n63 (comparing German and Dutch legal decisions); Queen Mary, University of London, International Arbitral Award Writing, <https://www.qmul.ac.uk/law/postgraduate/courses/short/arbitration-award-writing/> accessed 29 August 2019 (offering a course in award writing and indicating that the mock award produced by students must exceed 5,000 words). A somewhat shorter example can be found at *Consortium member* (Italy) *v Consortium leader* (Netherlands), Final Award, ICC Case No 14630 XXXVII *Yearbook Commercial Arbitration* 90 (2012). Notably, some commentators have suggested that "in some instances, longer is not better" when it comes to drafting arbitral awards. Born (n 2) 3041-42.
29. Ralf Michaels, "The Functional Method of Comparative Law", in Mathias Reiman and Reinhard Zimmerman (eds), *The Oxford Handbook of Comparative Law* (Oxford University Press 2006) 339, 342, 357.
30. Born (n 2) 2207-10; W Laurence Craig, "The Arbitrator's Mission and the Application of Law in International Commercial Arbitration", (2010) 21 American Review of International Law 243, 284; Strong, Judicial Guide (n 1) 6.
31. Daniel L FitzMaurice and Maureen O'Connor, "Preparing a Reasoned Award", (2007) 14 ARIAS US Quarterly; S.I. Strong, Katia Fach Gómez and Laura Carballo Piñeiro, *Comparative Law for Spanish-English Speaking Lawyers: Legal Cultures, Legal Terms and Legal Practices / Derecho comparado para abogados anglo- e hispanoparlantes: Culturas jurídicas, términos jurídicos y prácticas jurídicas* (Edward Elgar Publishing Ltd. 2016) 42-44, 49, 160-64.
32. Strong, *Judicial Guide* (n 1) 21.
33. Peter de Cruz, *Comparative Law in a Changing World* (Routledge-Cavendish 3d edn 2007) 70; Strong, Judicial Guide (n 1) 17.

34. S.I. Strong, *Research and Practice in International Commercial Arbitration: Sources and Strategies* (Oxford University Press 2009) 26-27 (Strong, *Research and Practice*); Interim Award in ICC Case Number 4131, IX Yearbook Commercial Arbitration 131, 135 (1984) ("The decisions of these [arbitral] tribunals progressively create caselaw which should be taken into account, because it draws conclusions from economic reality and conforms to the needs of international commerce, to which rules specific to international arbitration, themselves successively elaborated should respond."). The persuasive value of arbitral awards is highest in investment and sports arbitration, where such authorities provide a type of "soft precedent". Kaufmann-Kohler (n 13) 361-78.
35. JJ George, *Judicial Opinion Writing Handbook* (William S Hein and Co 5th edn 2007) 26. Providing all of the relevant factual data and outlining each step of the legal analysis allows an appellate court to consider the propriety of the decision-making process below in a comprehensive and principled manner. ibid.
36. Born (n 2) 83.
37. The right to appeal an arbitral award is found in section 69 of the Arbitration Act 1996, although parties may opt out of this provision. Arbitration Act 1996, s 69.
38. S.I. Strong, "Border Skirmishes: The Intersection Between Litigation and International Commercial Arbitration", 2012 *Journal of Dispute Resolution* 1, 2-6.
39. Born (n 2) 83. At one time, arbitrators were told to draft very terse awards lest they create grounds for vacatur or non-enforcement, an approach that some arbitrators still follow. Strong, *Legal Reasoning* (n 3) chs 3-4; Fontaine (n 22) 33. However, arbitrators are now advised to "protect the award" through judicious drafting, which may include a more detailed description of the reasons for the award. Strong, *Legal Reasoning* (n 3) chs 3-4; Edna Sussman, "Arbitrator Decision-Making: Unconscious Psychological Influences and What You Can Do About Them", (2014) XI *Revista Brasileira de Arbitragem* 76, 83.
40. Fontaine (n 22) 34; Herbert L Marx, Jr, "Who Are Labor Arbitration Awards Written For? And Other Musings About Award Writing", (May-July 2003) 58 Dispute Resolution Journal 2, 23 (quoting a party who stated, "We weren't at all happy with your award, but I can't complain because you explained it so well").
41. For example, an international arbitral tribunal that explicitly takes European competition or US antitrust law into account may dissuade a losing party from challenging an award in European or US courts on certain public policy grounds. Born (n 2) 3688-70 (discussing the "second look" doctrine); see also *Eco Swiss China Time Ltd v Benetton International NV*, [1999] ECR I-3055; *Mitsubishi Motors Corp v Soler Chrysler-Plymouth Inc*, 473 US 614, 638 (1985).
42. Born (n 2) 3732; Nadja Erk-Kabat, *Parallel Proceedings in International Arbitration: A European Perspective* (Wolters Kluwer 2014) 1; Strong, Judicial Guide (n 1) 85-87.
43. Born (n 2) 3733; Strong, *Judicial Guide* (n 1) 85-87.
44. Born (n 2) 3757.
45. American Arbitration Association (AAA), *Optional Appellate Arbitration Rules* (1 November 2013), <https://www.adr.org/sites/default/files/AAA-ICDR_Optional_Appellate_Arbitration_Rules.pdf> accessed 29 August 2019; International Institute for Conflict Prevention and Resolution (CPR) Arbitration Appeal Procedure and Commentary, <https://www.cpradr.org/resource-center/rules/arbitration/appellate-arbitration-procedure#> accessed 29 August 2019; JAMS, Optional Arbitration Appeal Procedure, <https://www.jamsadr.com/appeal/> accessed 29 August 2019; Arbitrators' and Mediators' Institute of New Zealand (AMINZ), Arbitration Appeals Tribunal, <https://www.aminz.org.nz/Category?Action=View&Category_id=173> accessed 29 August 2019.
46. For example, some questions exist as to whether and to what extent an appellate award can or should differ from an award at first instance as a matter of form or content. Strong, Reasoned Awards (n 12) 28-30; see also Born (n 2) 2926 (citing a French decision suggesting that in cases involving two tiers of arbitration, the first decision does not constitute an "award" per se).
47. The notion of what constitutes an appealable issue is by no means entirely clear. Paul Bennett Marrow, "A Practical Approach to Affording Review of Commercial Arbitration Awards Using an Appellate Arbitrator", (Aug-Oct 2005) 60 Dispute Resolution Journal 10, 14-15. At this point, parties must rely largely on the language reflected in the relevant rules.
48. Rudolph Kass, "A Private Path to Appellate Arbitration", (Jan/Feb 2006) 50 Boston Bar Journal 35, 35.
49. Gunnar Bergholtz, "*Ratio et Auctoritas*: A Comparative Study of the Significance of Reasoned Decisions with Special Reference to Civil Cases", (1989) 33 *Scandinavian Studies in Law* 11, 44.
50. Cohen (n 14) 532-33. This formulation can be compared to the test relating to the sufficiency of reasoning in arbitral awards. See nn 16-17 above and accompanying text.
51. Cohen (n 14) 532-33.

52. Catherine A. Rogers, "The Vocation of the International Arbitrator", (2005) 20 *American University International Law Review* 957, 985 n97.
53. Duarte Gorjão Henriques, "Motivation of Arbitral Awards: A Few Notes", (2013) 10 Young Arbitration Review 34, 34-35 (noting that arbitration awards must be reasoned under Portuguese law).
54. Strong, *Legal Reasoning* (n 3) ch 4.
55. For example, some commentators have suggested that arbitral awards do not necessarily need to have the same degree and depth of legal reasoning as judicial decisions and opinions. Born (n 2) 3044. However, empirical evidence suggests that many arbitral awards reflect a considerable amount of legal reasoning. Strong, *Legal Reasoning* (n 3) ch 5.
56. Humphrey Lloyd and others, "Drafting Awards in ICC Arbitration", (2005) 16 *ICC Court Bulletin* 19, 27.
57. See n 28 above and accompanying text.
58. George (n 35) 27; Fontaine (n 22) 34; Chad M. Oldfather, "Writing, Cognition, and the Nature of the Judicial Function", (2008) 96 *Georgetown Law Journal* 1283, 1302.
59. Richard A Posner, "Judges' Writing Styles (And Do They Matter?)", (1995) 62 *University of Chicago Law Review* 1421, 1447-48.
60. FitzMaurice and O'Connor (n 31) n19.
61. ibid; Alan Scott Rau, "Integrity in Private Judging", (1997) 38 *South Texas Law Review* 485, 532 (quoting Thomas Carbonneau for the proposition that "reasoned awards 'could serve as a means of assessing the arbitrators' ability to assure the parties of a principled decisional basis'" (citation omitted)); see also George (n 35) 26.
62. Hiro N Aragaki, "Arbitration's Suspect Status", (2011) 159 *University of Pennsylvania Law Review* 1233, 1263 (noting critics of arbitration often claim that arbitration results in "second-class justice"); Born (n 2) 821 n202; Catherine A. Rogers, "Transparency in International Commercial Arbitration", (2006) 54 *University of Kansas Law Review* 1301, 1325; S.I. Strong, "Truth in a Post-Truth Society: How Sticky Defaults, Status Quo Bias and the Sovereign Prerogative Influence the Perceived Legitimacy of International Arbitration", 2018 *University of Illinois Law Review* 533, 535-36.
63. Craig (n 30) 284; Yackee (n 2) 629.
64. Robert J. MacCoun, "Voice, Control, and Belonging: The Double-Edged Sword of Procedural Fairness", (2005) 1 *Annual Review of Law and Social Science* 171, 177.
65. Theodore Eisenberg and Michael Heise, "Plaintiphobia in State Courts? An Empirical Study of State Court Trials on Appeal", (2009) 38 *Journal of Legal Studies* 121, 126; Don Peters, "It Takes Two to Tango, and to Mediate: Legal Cultural and Other Factors Influencing United States and Latin American Lawyers' Resistance to Mediating Commercial Disputes", (2010) 9 *Richmond Journal of Law and Business* 391, 398 n124.
66. For more on the nature of the survey discussed in this Article, see nn 4-7 above and accompanying text.
67. Participants could also provide additional data through a write-in text box, and many did in fact mention the need to comply with requirements contained in arbitration agreements or arbitral rules. For a more detailed analysis of write-in comments, see Strong, *Legal Reasoning* (n 3) fig. 3.35.
68. Benjamin N. Cardozo, *The Nature of the Judicial Process* (Yale University Press 1949) 164-65.
69. Julie Bédard, "Transsystemic Teaching of Law at McGill: 'Radical Changes, Old and New Hats'", (2001) 27 *Queen's Law Journal* 237, 269-70; see also Roscoe Pound, "What Is the Common Law" in The Future of the Common Law (Harvard University Press 1937) 3, 18, as cited in Konrad Zweigert and Hein Kötz, An Introduction to Comparative Law (Tony Weir trans, 3rd edn, Oxford University Press 1998) 259. This issue is tested, to a limited degree, in Strong, *Legal Reasoning* (n 3) fig. 3.30.
70. See nn 58-60 above and accompanying text.
71. See nn 61-62 above and accompanying text.
72. See nn 63-68 above and accompanying text.
73. For example, unlike the civil law, which uses deductive reasoning to move from general principles of law to particular outcomes in specific cases, the common law uses analogical or inductive reasoning to generate general principles of law as a result of legal conclusions generated in large numbers of individual disputes. This approach has been said to be bottom-up, rather than top-down, which is the civil law method. Bédard (n 69) 269-70; see also Pound (n 69) 18. This issue is tested, to a limited degree, in Strong, *Legal Reasoning* (n 3) fig. 3.30.
74. Strong, Fach and Carballo (n 31) 46-56.

75. ibid.

76. Eg, de Cruz (n 33) 69; Zweigert and Kötz (n 69) 144.

77. Strong, *Research and Practice* (n 34) 12, 31-37; S.I. Strong, "Research in International Commercial Arbitration: Special Skills, Special Sources", (2009) 20 *American Review of International Arbitration* 119, 131-56 (Strong, Special Skills, Special Sources).

78. Strong, *Research and Practice* (n 34) 12, 31-37; Strong, Special Skills, Special Sources (n 77) 131-56.

79. For more on standard assumptions, see Vivienne O'Connor, *Common Law and Civil Law Traditions: Practitioner's Guide* (International Network to Promote the Rule of Law 2015) 11-15, <https://www.fjc.gov/sites/default/files/2015/Common%20and%20Civil%20Law%20Traditions.pdf> accessed 29 August 2019.

80. Guido Calabresi, *A Common Law for the Age of Statutes* (Harvard University Press 1982) 5-7; de Cruz (n 33) 70; Neal Devins and David Klein, "The Vanishing Common Law Judge?" (2017) 165 *University of Pennsylvania Law Review* 595, 597.

81. Some exceptions exist. Mary Garvey Algero, "The Sources of Law and the Value of Precedent: A Comparative and Empirical Study of a Civil Law State in a Common Law Nation", (2005) 65 *Louisiana Law Review* 775 (empirically studying the civil law legal system in Louisiana); Devins and Klein (n 80) 595 (empirically considering whether U.S. judges continue to use the common law method).

82. Strong, Legal Reasoning (n 3).

83. ibid.

84. O'Connor (n 79) 11-15; S.I. Strong, "Monism and Dualism in International Commercial Arbitration: Overcoming Barriers to Consistent Application of Principles of Public International Law", in Marko Novaković ed, *Basic Concepts of Public International Law: Monism and Dualism* (University of Belgrade 2013) 547, 549-50.

85. Notably, some confusion may have existed in the survey about the concept of soft law, which was intended to include arbitral rules. However, the survey question allowed participants to supplement their responses with additional written information in a text box, and a number of individuals indicated that they believed arbitral rules to be of central importance if the parties had adopted those rules. Strong, *Legal Reasoning* (n 3) ch 3. This suggests that some participants may have distinguished between different types of soft law in their responses. As a result, it may be helpful for researchers to develop targeted empirical studies that differentiate between various types of soft law in both substantive and procedural disputes.

86. It is possible that the fact that the survey was conducted in English increased the likelihood that civil law respondents had been influenced by common law thinking and/or by the unique norms that were applicable in international commercial arbitration. However, a not insignificant number of civil law respondents (21 per cent) indicated that they were focusing exclusively on domestic disputes, which suggests that the results cannot be attributed solely to the influence of common law thinking. ibid.

87. No statistical analyses were run on the relative ranking of responses within each cohort, so it cannot be said whether the differences were significant.

88. No statistical analyses were run on the relative ranking of responses between different questions.

89. The larger empirical study seeks to confirm some relevant behaviours. ibid. ch 5 (conducting a qualitative analysis of judicial decisions and arbitral awards).

90. ibid. fig. 3.39.

91. Strong, *Reasoned Awards* (n 12) 5-6 (citation omitted) (noting that US Supreme Court Justice Hugo Black once said that "the most difficult thing about coming on to the Court was learning to write"); see also William Domnarski, *In the Opinion of the Court* (University of Illinois Press 1997) 36; Emily Kadens, "The Puzzle of Judicial Education: The Case of Chief Justice William de Grey", (2009) 75 *Brooklyn Law Review* 143, 143.

92. Strong, Reasoned Awards (n 12) 5-6 (quoting Doug Jones, "Acquisition of Skills and Accreditation in International Arbitration", (2006) 22 *Arbitration international* 275, 281).

93. This trend can also be seen in the programs offered by various arbitral institutions. International Arbitration Information, International Arbitration Conferences <https://www.international-arbitration-attorney.com/international-arbitration-conferences/> accessed 29 August 2019.

94. Eg, Environmental Law Institute, Judicial Education Program <https://www.eli.org/judicial-education> accessed 29 August 2019; Law and Economics Center, Mason Judicial Education Program <https://masonlec.org/divisions/mason-judicial-education-program/> accessed 29 August 2019. The debate about for-profit judicial education programming has been vigorous. Center for Public Integrity, Corporations, Pro-Business Nonprofits Foot Bill for Judicial Seminars

(27 May 272014) <http://www.publicintegrity.org/2013/03/28/12368/corporations-pro-business-nonprofits-foot-bill-judicial-seminars> accessed 29 August 2019 (noting that "conservative foundations, multinational oil companies and a prescription drug maker were the most frequent sponsors of more than 100 expense-paid educational seminars attended by federal judges over a 4 1/2 year period"); Bruce A Green, "May Judges Attend Privately Funded Educational Programs? Should Judicial Education Be Privatized?: Questions of Judicial Ethics and Policy", (2002) 29 *Fordham Urban Law Journal* 941, 941-44.

95. Cheryl Thomas, Review of Judicial Training in Other Jurisdictions (UCL Judicial Institute May 2006) 8, 16 (discussing judicial writing programs around the world and noting the United States, Canada and Spain are leaders in judicial education, offering numerous courses in "judge craft", which includes judicial writing), <http://www.ucl.ac.uk/laws/judicial-institute/files/Judicial_Training_and_Education_in_other_Jurisdictions.pdf> accessed 29 August 2019; National Judicial Institute (Canada), Course Calendar <https://www.nji-inm.ca/index.cfm/publications/nji-education-course-calendar/> accessed 29 August 2019 (including a course calendar that discusses the "craft of judging", including judge craft, court craft and professional craft). Best practices in judicial education are discussed in various sources, including Judicial Education and Training, the official journal of the International Organization for Judicial Training.

96. Strong, Reasoned Awards (n 12) 7.

97. While a limited number of providers of judicial and arbitral education offer coursework in how to structure reasoned decisions and awards, recent empirical research suggests only about half (52 per cent) of judges and arbitrators have taken classes on how to write a reasoned decision or awards. Strong, *Legal Reasoning* (n 3) fig. 3.38. Notably, such classes—like virtually all forms of judicial and arbitral education—are voluntary rather than mandatory in nature. Strong, Reasoned Awards (n 12) 6-7 (noting availability of coursework on writing awards); Strong, "Reasoned Decisions" (n 12) 96 (noting availability of coursework on writing decisions).

98. Strong, *Legal Reasoning* (n 3) fig. 3.38.

99. While this was not one of the proffered responses, participants were able to provide additional alternatives in an open comment box. ibid fig. 3.41.

100. Jürgen Basedow, "Comparative Law and Its Clients", (2014) 62 *American Journal of Comparative Law* 821, 856.

101. ibid; Emmanuel Gaillard, "The Use of Comparative Law in International Commercial Arbitration", in Pieter Sanders (ed), *ICCA Congress Series Number 4: Arbitration in Settlement of International Commercial Disputes Involving the Far East and Arbitration in Combined Transport* (International Council for Commercial Arbitration 1989) 281, 281.

102. Additional information is available in Strong, *Legal Reasoning* (n 3).

103. The full chart and methodology are discussed in Strong, *Legal Reasoning* (n 3) fig. 3.35.

104. The full chart and methodology are discussed in Strong, *Legal Reasoning* (n 3) fig. 3.5.

105. The full chart and methodology are discussed in Strong, *Legal Reasoning* (n 3) fig. 3.6.

106. The full chart and methodology are discussed in Strong, *Legal Reasoning* (n 3) fig. 3.41.

Chapter 4
Show, Don't Tell: Creative Writing for Arbitrators

by Anja Ipp*

I. INTRODUCTION

> The widely accepted structure for arbitration awards is, from a storytelling perspective, absolute crap.
>
> —Bart Legum, GAR Live Stockholm 2018[1]

When you ask people in the arbitration industry—counsel, users, those working at institutions, even arbitrators themselves—how they feel about reading awards from cover to cover, most will sigh, chuckle, or roll their eyes. Reading awards is nobody's favourite part of the job.

We all know the feeling. You have agonised over written submissions, engaged in brain acrobatics to figure out how to build a sturdy case out of whatever evidence is available, and you missed your kids' soccer games to prepare for the hearing. Then, when the award is handed down, you open the last page to look at the operative part of the award. If you won, you make a couple of celebratory phone calls. If you lost, you go get a cup of coffee before sitting down to figure out why your case did not fly with the tribunal. After an hour or two, you have a headache but no idea on how to explain to the client why you lost. Did the tribunal really consider all your arguments? Why did they adopt the other side's interpretation of the contract? Why does the award say nothing about your star witness? Ok, I exaggerate slightly for effect here, but not that much.

My creative writing teacher at University of California Berkeley, Professor Jane, would scribble nuggets of writing advice in red ballpoint pen in the margins of our short stories: Think about the reader! Structure! Show, don't tell! Two decades later, I find myself wanting to do the same when I read arbitration awards. There has been plenty of discussion in the arbitration community about the need to write better awards. But what are the characteristics of a good award? Is it all about including more in-depth reasoning? And how much can arbitrators really deviate from the standard format and language?

The aim of this brief article is to suggest some answers to these questions, drawing on my five years at the Arbitration Institute of the Stockholm Chamber of Commerce and my background as a writer and editor. Having read (or tried to read) hundreds of awards, I argue that there is room for improvement, innovation and creativity in award writing.

* Legal Counsel, Arbitration Institute of the Stockholm Chamber of Commerce (SCC)

II. BACKGROUND

While arbitration may not be an industry known for its proclivity for innovation and out-of-the-box thinking, the community of arbitration professionals have embraced quite a bit of change over the past few years. In its infancy, expedited arbitration raised serious due process concerns, but is now challenging "regular" arbitration in terms of popularity. The emergency arbitrator procedure was similarly regarded with scepticism when first introduced by the SCC in 2010, but less than a decade later it is offered by all major institutions and widely accepted and used by parties. Most recently on the innovation front, the SCC launched a digital platform for the online administration of cases by tribunals and parties. These are merely a few of many trends and developments showing that arbitration is constantly evolving, and that the arbitration community is open and willing to embrace new practices, models and ideas. Perhaps it is time that this openness be extended to the way in which we draft our end products: the arbitral awards.

I posit that an arbitration is only as good as the final award. While efficiency, expeditiousness and procedural fairness are important, it is the award that is the true measure of quality in arbitration. Excellent procedural management will not make up for an unsatisfactory award, but most parties will probably excuse the tribunal's delays if the award is clear and convincing. For arbitral institutions, most of whom have limited control over the content and format of the final product, this means that the ultimate measure of quality of the service that we provide is in the hands of the arbitrators. Yet there is scarce guidance on how to write a good award; arbitrators are largely on their own when it comes to presenting their decisions and explaining how they arrived at their conclusions.

Most arbitration rules include a requirement that the tribunal should include in the award the reasons for its decisions. In the SCC Arbitration Rules ("SCC Rules"), this language is found in Art 42(1): "The Arbitral Tribunal shall make its award in writing, and, unless otherwise agreed by the parties, shall state the reasons upon which the award is based."[2] Beyond that, the SCC and other arbitration rules provide no guidance as to the structure of the award, or the required or desired depth or format of the tribunal's reasoning.

Institutional guidelines and practice notes for arbitrators do not go much further in telling arbitrators how to present their findings and decisions.[3] The LCIA Notes for Arbitrators and the ICC Note to Parties and Arbitral Tribunals on the Conduct of the Arbitration are silent on the content and structure of the award.[4] The same was true for the SCC Arbitrators' Guidelines until the most recent revision, when some pointers were added to help arbitrators think about award structure and perhaps avoid the most common award-writing pitfalls.[5] The Guidelines do not, however, go as far as suggesting a complete makeover along the lines I sketch out in this article.

Most rules also include an umbrella stipulation requiring the tribunal to "make every reasonable effort to ensure that any award is legally enforceable."[6] Depending on the seat, arbitrators may thus find some guidance in the applicable arbitration law and look to the courts for guidance on what constitutes "reasons" under the arbitration rules. In most arbitration-friendly jurisdictions, however, the bar for reasons is extremely low; a mere modicum of reasoning is enough for the award to be enforceable. As explained by the Supreme Court of Sweden:

> Providing sufficient legal reasons in an arbitral award is a guardian of the rule of law, as it forces the arbitrators to analyze the legal issues and submitted evidence... [However,] challenge proceedings do not grant grounds for a test of the merits of the arbitral tribunal's conclusions. As a result of the foregoing, and having regard to the difficulties with respect to scope that a qualitative review of the reasons would cause, **only a total lack of reasons, or reasons that are so lacking that they can be equated to a total lack of reasons, can constitute a procedural error.**[7]

In other words, the courts will not evaluate the quality or sufficiency of an arbitrator's reasoning. Moreover, arbitration institutions provide limited guidance, if any. What does this low bar and poor road map mean for the arbitrators? It means freedom. Freedom to be innovative, creative and write the best award possible in every arbitration.

III. THE PARALLELS BETWEEN STORYTELLING AND AWARD WRITING

It may seem at first glance that award writing has nothing in common with—or to learn from—the creative writing genre. Creative writing is about making up a story that will entertain and engage the reader emotionally; in arbitration awards we try to do the opposite, right? We do *not* make stuff up, and our ambition is limited to delivering one or more decisions based on black-letter law, precedent and sound legal and factual analysis. Entertainment or manipulation of feelings is not among the tribunal's ambitions.

But what is a story, really? Professor Jane, my Berkeley writing teacher, would tell you that a story is a piece of writing that contains five elements: *setting, plot, characters, conflict* and *theme.* It is by skilfully weaving these elements together that an author allows the action to develop in a logical way that the reader can follow. A story begins with exposition of the setting and the central characters, then the plot develops through rising action and conflict—conflict between characters or forces is at the centre of every story—that builds up to a climax. At the end of the story, there is always resolution, meaning that the central conflict that constituted the main plotline has been resolved. Finally, the *theme* of the story is its moral, its message, the bigger idea that the story illustrates about society or human nature—or perhaps about business.

Do you see the parallels? Arbitrations are stories, really. The tribunal and parties are the *characters,* and the *setting* is the business or contractual relationship between them. The *plot* develops when things go sour in the parties' relationship, perhaps goods are not delivered as agreed or the parties have different interpretations of an earn-out provision, and when the parties are unable to agree on a way forward, this reveals the central *conflict.* The arbitration ends, as do most stories, with the eventual resolution of that central conflict. The *theme*, then, is what the dispute says about a specific area of law, or how it illustrates the difficulties of certain business ventures or relationships.

If arbitration has all the elements of a story, perhaps we could think of award writing as story telling? Writing a good award becomes an exercise of skilfully telling the story of the parties' relationship, the dispute between them, and how the tribunal resolved that dispute in a fair and convincing way.

IV. PRINCIPLES OF CREATIVE WRITING APPLIED TO ARBITRATION

Aware of the story-like features of the arbitrations before them, arbitrators may consider looking to the field of creative writing for inspiration and guidance on to write the best possible award. In this section I discuss a few key principles of storytelling that translate particularly well to the arbitration context, and that I believe could serve arbitrators in the award writing process. Those principles are (1) Think about the reader, (2) The three-act structure, and (3) Show, don't tell.

IV.A. Think About the Reader

Professor Jane would repeatedly emphasise the point that creative writers *serve* their readers; the reader should always be the writer's most important consideration. A writer must skilfully wield the tools in the literary toolbox—balancing the elements of setting, plot, characters, conflict and theme—to keep the readers interested, engaged and invested in the story. To do this, writers must know and understand who the readers are and what they want or need from the story. In other words, who are you writing for and why?

Arbitrators should ask themselves the same questions. Before putting pen to paper, or fingertips to keyboard, the arbitrator must think about the reader: For whom am I writing the award, and what do they need from me? Taking care to know and think about the audience this way, the arbitrator can tailor the presentation of decisions and reasoning to best serve the parties.

It is often said that the reasoning in an arbitral award is primarily for the losing party, to make him understand why he lost.[8] A well written arbitral award is an award that leaves the losing party feeling heard and satisfied that the tribunal considered its evidence and understood its arguments. Why do we care about the losing party's feelings? Because a satisfied—albeit disappointed—loser is unlikely to pick apart the award and the arbitration process looking for grounds on which to base a challenge. A party who understands why he lost will perceive the arbitral process as fair and desirable, which serves not only the continuing vitality of arbitration, but also the arbitrator looking for future appointments.[9]

On the side of the losing party, the ultimate readers of the award are likely to be business people—the project manager rather than the in-house counsel of a party, let alone the external counsel.[10] These business people have to understand, and hopefully perceive as convincing, how the arbitral tribunal reached its conclusions on the issues with which they are familiar—that is, primarily the facts.[11] Keeping in mind throughout the award writing process that the primary audience is business people on the losing side should encourage arbitrators to demonstrate how they reached their decisions, and to avoid overly legal language.

Based on scores of awards read during my half-decade with the SCC, I would say that one of the keys to writing a "loser-friendly" award is carefully *weighing* the parties' evidence and arguments against each other. This may seem obvious. But consider the basic structure of many arbitration awards: (1) claimant's version of the facts and interpretation of the contract; (2) respondent's version of the same thing, and (3) tribunal's version of the same thing. The problem with this model is that (3) at best *explains* the tribunal's own interpretation of the contract or the disputed events. The tribunal often fails to explicitly assess the relative merit of (1) and (2), balancing them against each other and showing why one comes out on top. Too often, arbitrators present their findings and explanations as the objective truth and leave the reader to figure out with whom they agreed and why.

In contrast, a tribunal who thinks of the audience—primarily the losing party—will take care to explain how the process of weighing the parties' submissions against each other resulted in the conclusions reached. Doing so means explicitly referencing the parties' arguments and evidence on specific issues, explaining the applicable legal test or standard, and then explicitly applying that test or standard to the parties' submissions. What losing parties want and need from the award is to understand why the tribunal did not agree with their version of what happened, or their interpretation of the contract or circumstances. A tribunal that thinks about its audience like the creative writer thinks about the reader will cater for the loser's needs by specifically addressing the losing party's central arguments or submissions, acknowledging their relative merit, and then explaining why the tribunal nonetheless came down on the other side. As put by Chinese arbitration practitioner Arthur Ma at a recent panel discussion:

> The tribunal has the mission to convince the parties where they are right and where they are wrong. In a sense, a tribunal, in drafting the award, is no different perhaps from the parties drafting the submissions when they were trying to convince the tribunal to accept their point. At the end of the day, all the parties of course hope they can win, but the award is drafted for the losing side. You have to convince the losing side why they lost the case; why they lost the factual point; why they lost the legal point. You can't just say, as in the example I just mentioned, that because there is no substantial written evidence, all the witness statements are rejected. I think that is not a good way to convince the losing side. The losing side will be so disappointed, especially when they receive the bill from the arbitrators. As legal service providers, we are engaged by the clients and we need to give them attention; **that's why they pay our bills**.[12]

At arbitration institutions such as SCC, we constantly think about the end users of arbitration—the business people that not only pay the bills for the arbitration, but who have the power to include or not to include an SCC arbitration clause in the next contract they enter into. *They* are our audience, those we consider to be the primary readers of arbitration awards, and who must be convinced of the outcome and the fairness of the proceedings, even if they lose.

IV.B. Structure: The Three Acts

As arbitration expert Bart Legum expressed in the quote at the beginning of this article, "the widely accepted structure for arbitration awards is, from a storytelling perspective, absolute crap." Sitting in the audience at the GAR Live event where Legum made this pointed remark, I noticed the familiar snicker of reluctant agreement spread among the rows of gray-suited shoulders. Many in the arbitration community dislike the current standard model according to which most awards are structured, yet continue to use that same model. But as we explored above, arbitrators have broad creative freedom when it comes to award writing; courts and institutions will not force an arbitrator's hand. Those who dare may rethink the traditional way of structuring awards, and draw some lessons from storytelling.

Most stories are told in three parts, or acts:

First, the set-up. This is where the writer establishes the setting, the characters, and relationships between them. Sometimes the writer starts with an attention-grabbing opening—perhaps a question, a vivid picture created in the reader's mind, or a flash-forward of an event to which the story builds up. Within the first act there is an *inciting incident,* the initial disturbance or dramatic occurrence involving the principal characters that sets everything in motion. In trying to deal with the inciting incident, the characters bring about the first turning point in the story, and reveal the central conflict.

Second, the confrontation. The turning point in the previous act becomes the central conflict or problem, which the characters attempt to resolve. Though *rising action,* the main character develops the knowledge, skills or character necessary to overcome the central problem—solve the murder, save the marriage, or find what was lost. Readers follow along through clues that show cause and effect.

Third, the resolution, or falling action. This is the climax of the story, where the central problem is overcome or the conflict resolved, and loose ends are tied up.

As we noted above, arbitrations have a lot in common with stories—we have a setting, a plot, characters, and resolution of a central conflict. Yet the structure of an arbitral award has little in common with the three-act structure of a story. In the first "act" of an arbitral award there is a lot of procedural details that have little to do with the dispute itself, plus an introduction of the setting, some of the characters, and the relationship between them. In the second "act", the claimant first takes us through the entire plotline, explaining the facts and disputed issues. Then, still in the second act, we go through the entire plotline again, this time from the respondent's perspective. In the third "act", and only in the third, usually more than halfway through the award, the tribunal steps onto the stage to give its version of the story. This structure is quite cumbersome. The reader is tossed hither and thither, and often must do a lot of work to follow along the plotline to the resolution of the central conflict.

In a story, the main character—the protagonist—is the one who resolves the story's central conflict. In an arbitration, the tribunal resolves the central conflict, but does not appear as the protagonist in the story, and in fact enters the stage only in the third act. Why? The purpose of the arbitral award is for the tribunal to render and explain its decisions, yet the tribunal waits backstage for the first two acts. The primary audience, the business people on the losing side, would probably be better served if the tribunal assumed the role of a protagonist narrator, who guided the story from beginning to end. The current practice of using copy-paste to let the parties tell their own parallel versions of the story is not an effective way to engage readers. We all know that.

A bold tribunal may open the first act with an attention-grabbing opening—perhaps even put the operative part of the award at the very beginning, like a flash-forward to which the story then builds up (and we all read the operative part first anyway). The protagonist tribunal would then describe the setting in which the arbitration took place, introduce the parties and the relationship between them. This would include all the undisputed facts and the circumstances, told by the tribunal in its own words. But beware! The tribunal must not distort the facts to support its conclusions. In the words of Lord Bingham, one of the great judges in English history:

> The judge must try and create a coherent and intelligible narrative, but he must ensure that his summaries do not distort. He must not avoid mention of events of which any party reasonably attaches significance, even if that significance is not in his view very great and he should definitely not slant the facts to suit his eventual conclusion. Nothing more quickly undermines confidence in a judgment than a sloppy, incoherent, inaccurate and partial account of events.[13]

Towards the end of the first act, the tribunal would describe the "inciting incident"—the point in the parties' relationship where things went wrong, a deadline was missed, or products failed to meet contract specifications. The central conflict would be revealed as the tribunal accounts for the parties' diverging views on the inciting incident, using specific references to their submissions and arguments.

Once the central conflict is revealed, the second act begins. Through what storytelling calls *confrontation,* the tribunal would develop the knowledge necessary to resolve the central conflict. In other words, this would be the "Sherlock Holmes" part, where the tribunal analyses the dispute between the parties. The point here is to *analyse* the disputed issues, not to *justify* the tribunal's decision (more about this in the next section). When all disputed issues have been analysed, that would mark the end of the second act.

The third act is then the climax of the story, where the central conflict is resolved. Here, the tribunal would weigh up the conclusions reached in the second act and deliver its final decision on the parties' dispute. When delivering the decision, arbitrators who think about the reader may wish to recount the losing party's strongest arguments and offer them some credit. This serves to leave the losing party feeling heard, more satisfied with the arbitration process, and hopefully less likely to challenge the award. For most arbitrations, where the central conflict is really about liability, the issue of quantum would probably come in the third act, as part of the wind-down. After that, the plotline has reached its end, and the tribunal ties up loose ends by ruling on apportionment of costs. If the tribunal did not use the operative part of the award as an attention-grabbing opening, it would also be included at the end.

Where is the procedural history in this storytelling award? Well, to the extent that it is part of the setting, it could be included in the first act. Another idea, which the arbitration community floats now and then, is to move the history to an annex, removing the burden of excessive procedural detail from the narrative flow. I doubt any reviewing court would set aside an arbitral award based on placement of the procedural history. Also, we should keep in mind that "procedural history" does not have to include everything; the fact that a respondent filed an English translation of Exhibit C-6 on June 15 has no bearing on a court's review of the award.

IV.C. Show, Don't Tell

> Don't tell me the moon is shining; show me the glint of light on the broken glass. —Anton Chekov, Russian 19th century writer

"Show, don't tell" is a central principle of storytelling, a classic piece of writing advice that has been handed down from generation to generation of writers. Yet it can be elusive, hard to grasp, and difficult to apply in practice. What does it mean to *show* and how does one do it?

Consider the experience of reading that a character is a mean person (telling) versus reading a description of that same character kicking a dog (showing). How about "he was nervous" (telling) versus "he tapped his fingers on the tabletop" (showing)? Or "Polly loved to dive into her swimming pool" (telling) versus "With clumsy jubilance, Polly hurled her body from the rattling board and surfaced grinning through the kelp of her own hair" (showing).[14] As Professor Jane would explain, a skilled writer does not tell the reader what to see or what to think, but rather conveys the intended image or message by scenes, description and clues. We all prefer witnessing an event to hearing about it afterwards. This is why master editor Sol Stein urges writers to "show a story" instead of "tell a story." According to Stein, "One of the chief reasons why novels are rejected is that the writer, consciously or not, is reporting a story instead of showing it."[15]

It may not be obvious how to apply "show, don't tell" in the drafting of an arbitration award, where clarity is of paramount importance, and where we are less concerned with the reader's experience than with his or her understanding of our conclusions. Well, perhaps there is a way to accomplish both. Let us look at some examples of "telling" in the arbitration context: "In the opinion of the arbitral tribunal, there is no doubt that" and "in the opinion of the tribunal, the respondent had good reasons for [acting as it did]".[16] We also see arbitrators stating that "the investigation has shown" this or that, or that "there is evidence that supports" a certain conclusion, without showing the reader anything about the details of that investigation or where in the record we can find the evidence. These are all instances of arbitrators telling the parties what the arbitrators have concluded. Does this type of language serve to convince our primary reader, a business person on the losing side, that our conclusions are correct and well-reasoned?

Instead, "showing" in the arbitration context means to present and evaluate the parties' evidence and analyse their arguments in a systematic, reader-friendly fashion—a sort of rising action that builds up to the climax of the story, where the tribunal presents its decisions based on the foregoing analysis. Consider the subtle but very important difference between analysis and reasons; analysis shows the reader how the tribunal *arrived at* its conclusion, whereas reasons *justify* that same conclusion. Analysis precedes the decision and is more conducive to "showing", whereas reasons come after the decision has been made and is more likely to involve "telling". Accordingly, arbitrators concerned with convincing the audience that the decision is fair and correct—and thereby reducing the risk of challenges to the award and increasing the chances of future appointments—may want to shift their perspective away from reasons and move towards a greater focus on analysis. In practice, this means, in the second "act" of the award, introducing each disputed issue, clearly stating the applicable legal rule or standard, applying that rule or standard to the parties' arguments and evidence, and arriving at the conclusion. Through analysis, the tribunal shows the parties how the story's central conflict is resolved.

Finally, a few words about language. The vocabulary, sentence structure and tone required for "showing" may be more descriptive, colourful, and informal than what we are used to seeing in arbitral awards. This may make us uncomfortable, since most of us are used to combine sophisticated words into complex sentences with a formal tone. But perhaps we must question that discomfort, and ask ourselves why we insist on writing like lawyers when our primary audience consists of business people? Arbitrators are not judges, and there is no requirement that they write like judges. In fact, there is often nothing forcing judges to write like judges, other than tradition and expectation. I will let master editor Sol Stein make my point for me:

> [J]ust because people work for an institution, they don't have to write like one. Institutions can be warmed up. Administrators can be turned into human beings. Information can be imparted clearly and without pomposity. You only have to remember that readers identify with people. Not with abstractions like "profitability," or with Latinate nouns like "utilization" and "implementation," or inert constructions in which nobody can be visualized doing something: pre-feasibility study in the paperwork stage.[17]

V. CONCLUSION

In case you approached this article like a typical arbitration award and skipped straight to the operative part—Welcome! In the preceding pages, I have concluded that:

The reasoning in most awards meet the requirements set by applicable arbitration law and rules, yet most of us cringe at the thought of reading an award from beginning to end;

Arbitrations contain all the elements of a story, namely setting, characters, plot, conflict, and theme; and

Arbitrators will write better awards if they apply some principles of effective storytelling. Specifically:

Think about the reader. The primary audience of the arbitral award are the business people on the losing side. If they understand why they lost, they are unlikely to challenge the award, and likely to include arbitration clauses in their contracts.

Use a three-act structure. The standard model for arbitral awards is cumbersome. Readers can more easily follow a plotline from set-up to resolution if it is clearly narrated by the tribunal, with references to the parties' evidence and arguments.

Show, don't tell. Analysis shows readers how the tribunal arrived at its conclusion, whereas reasons justify that same conclusion. They are more likely to agree with the conclusion if we showed them the way there.

Now, if you have the time and the inclination, go get a cup of coffee and flip back to the section that looks more interesting. See you there.

NOTES

1. Remarks by Bart Legum, GAR Live Stockholm *Lookback: how to write an arbitral award*, 17 May 2019, available at https://globalarbitrationreview.com/article/1193111/gar-live-stockholm-lookback-how-to-write-an-arbitral-award
2. cf. Art 32(2) of the ICC Rules; Art. 34(2) of the UNCITRAL Rules; Art 26.2 of the LCIA Rules (2014).
3. See Felix Dasser and Emmanuel O. Igbokwe, "The Award and the Courts, Efficient Drafting of the Arbitral Award: Traditional Ways Revisited—Lesson Learned from the Past?", in Christian Klausegger, Peter Klein , et al. (eds), *Austrian Yearbook on International Arbitration 2019*, pp. 280-81.
4. https://www.lcia.org/adr-services/lcia-notes-for-arbitrators.aspx#6.7%20The%20Award
5. https://sccinstitute.com/media/1067295/scc-guidelines-for-arbitrators.pdf
6. Art. 2(2) of the SCC Rules.
7. Decision of the Supreme Court of Sweden, 31 March 2009, Case No. T 4387-07/NJA 2009 s. 128, available at https://www.arbitration.sccinstitute.com/Swedish-Arbitration-Portal/Supreme-Court/The-Supreme-Court2/The-Supreme-Court/d_1023208-decision-of-the-supreme-court-of-sweden-31-march-2009-case-no.-t-4387-07nja-2009-s.-128?search=hochtieff
8. The winning party, while less inclined to read every word of the award, may still be interested in the arbitral tribunal's reasoning to the extent that it affects the winning party's business going forward. Perhaps the tribunal's reasoning causes the party to reconsider its General Terms and Conditions or to restructure certain agreements to remove ambiguities and avoid expensive arbitrations in the future. See Felix Dasser and Emmanuel O. Igbokwe, "The Award and the Courts, Efficient Drafting of the Arbitral Award: Traditional Ways Revisited—Lesson Learned from the Past?", in Christian Klausegger, Peter Klein , et al. (eds), *Austrian Yearbook on International Arbitration 2019*, pp. 285.
9. R. Doak Bishop, "The Quality of Arbitral Decision-Making and Justification", *World Arbitration & Mediation Review* vol 7:1 (2013) at 250.
10. Remarks by Philipp Habegger, GAR Live Stockholm Lookback: how to write an arbitral award, 17 May 2019, available at https://globalarbitrationreview.com/article/1193111/gar-live-stockholm-lookback-how-to-write-an-arbitral-award
11. id.
12. Remarks by Arthur Ma, "GAR Live Stockholm Lookback: how to write an arbitral award", 17 May 2019, available at https://globalarbitrationreview.com/article/1193111/gar-live-stockholm-lookback-how-to-write-an-arbitral-award
13. R. Doak Bishop, "The Quality of Arbitral Decision-Making and Justification", *World Arbitration & Mediation Review* vol 7:1 (2013) at 246.
14. See Sol Stein, "Stein on Writing: A Master Editor of Some of the Most Successful Writers of Our Century Shares his Craft Techniques and Strategies", St. Martin's Griffin (1995) at 124-26.
15. See Sol Stein, "Stein on Writing: A Master Editor of Some of the Most Successful Writers of Our Century Shares his Craft Techniques and Strategies", *St. Martin's Griffin* (1995) at 123.
16. These specific wordings are pulled from a relatively recent award where three senior arbitrators dismissed claims totalling EUR 40 million.
17. William Zinsser, "On Writing Well: The Classic Guide to Writing Nonfiction", *Harper Quill* (2001) at 166-167.

Chapter 5

Reasons in International Commercial and Investment Arbitration Awards

How Much and How?

by Luca G. Radicati di Brozolo*

I. INTRODUCTION

I intend to raise a few questions on specific points regarding what should go into an award, and how it is to be said.

We all know what the reasons for providing reasons for arbitral awards are. Probably the most important one is to oblige the arbitrators to think carefully of every aspect of the dispute and to allow them to come to a decision that is fully thought through and respectful of the rules by which they have to abide in reaching their decision, and that has the cogency, intellectual rigour and persuasiveness that only writing can provide. Related to this is the need to ensure fairness and due process and avoiding arbitrariness or even just loose thinking. Other reasons are to explain to the losing party why it lost and to strengthen the legitimacy of a decision rendered by individuals who exercise a judicial function without any public authority and, moreover, whose decisions are subject only to very limited review.

These reasons apply both to commercial arbitration and to investor-State arbitration. In investor-State arbitration there is at least one additional reason, which is to clarify the law and possibly to contribute to its development, as well as to promote consistency and predictability. The need for convincing and elaborate reasoning is particularly strong in investor-State arbitration at a time when the appropriateness of having private arbitrators deciding disputes involving affairs of State is under severe and (to put it mildly) not benevolent scrutiny.

It is useful to note that the problem of the reasoning of the award is, at least conceptually, different from that of the decision-making process. The decision—and therefore laying down the rule that settles the dispute brought to arbitration—is obviously the principal task of the arbitrators. In this connection there are multiple issues: what rules and principles should the arbitrators apply and how should they go about ascertaining their content, how should they assess the evidence, should they simply act as referees between the parties and choose between their competing arguments or do they have to perform a higher function of administering justice or finding the truth, should they strive to ensure some form of consistency with other arbitral case law (this is certainly more a concern in

* Founding Partner, Arblit; Professor at the School of Law of the Università Cattolica di Milano

investor-State arbitration, but may not be totally out of place in commercial arbitration) and so on. One could call this the intellectual process of reaching this decision.

At least in the sense in which the term is generally used in this context, the reasoning is the explanation and making explicit of the intellectual path followed by the decision-maker to come to its decision. Strictly speaking, a reasoning in this sense is not required for a decision, and in fact awards can in principle be unreasoned. This was actually very often the case in older days. However, in modern arbitration—both commercial and investor-State—reasoning is viewed as indispensable for the reasons mentioned above, and it must now be in writing. This is consistent with the fact that arbitration is no longer limited to the settlement of minor technical disputes as was primarily the case at the origin, but is a full-blown alternative to the judicial process (and often actually the only option) for the settlement of important disputes.

The question we are asked to focus on is how this explanation of the grounds of the decision is to be done. Although the term reasoning is usually referred only to the part of the award that deals expressly with the grounds for the decision, I think it is useful to consider, albeit more succinctly, all the other parts of the award, since everything that goes into the text of the award is relevant to explain the thought process by which the arbitrators arrive at their decision.

I will adopt a practical approach, which goes essentially to the technique of drafting an award.

There are obviously a number of elementary requirements that apply to any type of award, things such clarity, logic, consistency, avoidance of ambiguities (and to the extent possible, repetitions), a decent use of grammar, syntax and language: those are the essentials required to render intelligible whatever the arbitrators intend to say. Beyond this there are many other ingredients to writing an award.

Basically, the main issue is: what, and how much, should the arbitrators say, and how should they say it? What questions must the arbitral tribunal ask itself and address when going about drafting an award?

This question is common to commercial and investor-State arbitration, although the approach and the solutions may not be the same in the two cases. And clearly there is no single way to answer it and each tribunal has its own way of writing an award, which may also vary from one arbitration to another depending on a variety of factors. These will include the nature, the importance and the complexity of the dispute and of the individual legal and factual issues raised by it as well as the energy and resources expended by the parties and their counsel. Other factors may be the nature of the review to which the award is subject and the level of publicity that the award may ultimately have.

The arbitrators will obviously also have to give consideration to the tension between the exhaustiveness and completeness of an award and the pressure to ensure the efficiency and speed of arbitration and the control of costs. One criticism often heard is that awards are too verbose. Is this always a fair criticism?

The problem of what and how to say things applies to all the parts of the award: the procedural history, the description of the facts, the arguments of the parties and, most importantly, to the specific arguments based on which the Tribunal reaches its decision. I will mention briefly the first ones and concentrate on the actual reasoning.

II. THE PRELIMINARY PARTS OF THE AWARD

The **procedural history** is clearly the most boring part of the final award, the one arbitrators find most tedious to write and the one nobody tends to read, except in case of a challenge. It is also the simplest to write, partly because it is the one that most easily lends itself to be delegated to assistants and secretaries. The question is whether too much effort is spent writing the procedural history, and whether this sometimes constitutes a disproportionate part of the final award. One of the culprits of the prolixity may be arbitral institutions, including ICC, which seem to insist on every single incident and piece of correspondence being mentioned.

There is however no doubt that the rehearsal of the procedural history has considerable importance, particularly to ensure that all procedural requirements (in particular due process) were respected. Moreover, for the tribunal, reviewing the procedural history in detail can sometimes serve to bring back to memory aspects of the case that may continue to be relevant even at the end of the proceedings but may have been forgotten during the course of the arbitration.

In some cases it may be appropriate to devote a specific section of the award, which may be part of the procedural history or a section on its own, to issues of due process. This may make sense in case of particularly contentious proceedings rife with accusations of breach of due process by one or all parties. A detailed treatment of this aspect may help protect the award in case of challenge on that ground. I have personally experienced the usefulness of this in a case of mine, where a specific section of the award on due process was heavily relied upon by the court to reject a challenge to enforcement on that ground. Of course, this issue may already be the subject of procedural orders issued in the course of the proceedings, but consolidating it in the award may have its usefulness. Obviously the need for this exercise will depend on the circumstances.

The **facts section** is clearly of extreme importance. It is indeed essential that the arbitrators have, and be seen to have, a complete and detailed understanding and control of all the facts and evidence relating to them. Setting them out in detail in the award may be a way not only to ensure the reader that the arbitrators have properly understood the facts but, more importantly, to oblige the tribunal to look at them with the requisite attention.

As for all sections of the award, the challenge is striking the right balance between prolixity and conciseness or, put otherwise, between exhaustiveness and relevance. At the end of the process it may become clear that certain facts are irrelevant for the result. Should they nonetheless be recounted by the arbitrators just to show that they have not overlooked them, even if ultimately, for a good reason, they were not considered relevant and do not support the reasoning?

Essentially the same considerations apply to **the arguments of the parties**, which set out their vision of the facts and of the law, and are usually the subject of a specific section.

One practical question, that applies to both the discussion of the facts and of the parties' arguments, is whether these should be treated exhaustively in the initial sections respectively devoted to them, or whether those sections should only provide a less detailed, more bird's eye review of them, leaving a more specific discussion in the specific sections of the reasoning proper for which they are relevant. In my view, the second solution has the advantage of allowing the reader to obtain a general understanding of the dispute, without getting lost in excessive detail. It may also have the advantage of avoiding too much repetition, since the reasoning will usually require addressing the specific facts and party arguments that are relevant for each one of its passages.

III. THE REASONING

The actual reasoning is obviously the most important part, the core of the award, which builds on the material of the previous sections.

It goes without saying that this part has to be very precise and clear, and must allow the reader to understand exactly the reasons for which the arbitrators arrived at their decision. This implies that, at a minimum, the reasoning must address and explain all the arguments that are directly necessary to support the decision reflected in the dispositive part of the award. Very importantly, it must avoid contradictions between different parts of the reasoning, and between the reasoning and the dispositive.

This, however, leaves unanswered many questions that come to mind when setting about drafting an award.

The first one is that of the level of detail with which these essential arguments should be treated. The answer may be in some way similar to another particularly delicate question. This is whether the arbitrators should adopt a minimalistic approach by addressing only the arguments (or claims or defences) strictly necessary to come to their decision, or whether they should adopt a more comprehensive approach and discuss arguments, claims and defences and factual or legal points that go beyond what is strictly necessary. The bare statement that the tribunal has considered all the parties' arguments even if it has not specifically alluded to them may not be sufficient.

Sometimes the decision on a given point or claim or defence, or even on the entire dispute, can be reached without addressing all of the arguments raised by the parties. Should the arbitrators nevertheless also consider some or all of those arguments? The paradigmatic examples are jurisdiction and statute of limitations, but there are many more.

The easy answer would be that arbitrators should avoid going beyond the strictly indispensable. It is faster, more efficient. And one could say: least said, soonest mended.

Obviously, nobody would probably argue that the tribunal should even touch upon the merits if its decision is going to be that it has no jurisdiction (unless the merits are in some way intertwined with and necessary to decide on jurisdiction). However, the example of statute of limitations may be different. A tribunal might be uneasy relying simply on what, at least in some cases, may appear to be a formalistic argument. Its unease might be even greater if the decision on the decisive preliminary argument is based on an interpretation of the relevant rules which is not undisputed or is even hotly contested (perhaps even the governing law may be the subject of uncertainty or disagreement), and even more so if the decision is not unanimous (regardless of whether there is a formal dissent).

There are many other situations where the parties have discussed a host of factual and legal arguments that may justify a comprehensive analysis and an "even if" type of reasoning showing that the same result would be achieved also on other considerations. This can assist in giving comfort to the tribunal, bolstering the correctness of the final outcome and rendering the award more persuasive, strengthening it in case of challenge and giving the losing party the comfort that it has not lost on a mere technicality. Parties may be more prepared to accept an unfavourable decision based on a curt and formalistic argument from a court than from arbitrators.

Matters obviously stand differently if the arguments, beyond those which allow the tribunal to come to a certain result, go in a different direction. In that case it would evidently be foolish to address them and to say that, but for the winning arguments, the outcome would be different. It would clearly weaken the award.

In considering whether to stick to the bare minimum that allows them to come to a decision or to expand their reasoning, and in deciding what more to say and how to say it, arbitrators must take into account a variety of other factors. Efficiency and speed are only one consideration, albeit an important one. Arbitrators must be able to gauge what is expected of them from the addressees of the award and to give satisfactory answers, not only in terms of the strict factual and legal basis of the decision. The applicable law or rules will usually provide little or no guidance since they typically prescribe simply that the reasons should be adequate. Article 47(1)(i) of the ICSID Rules is an exception in that it goes a little further by dictating that the award deals with "every question submitted", but this too is far from providing an exhaustive answer to the problems on the table.

If the dispute is simple and without broader implications, and even more so if it is low value, and the pleadings have not been particularly sophisticated, it is reasonable to assume that the parties do not expect an elaborate decision, so that a bare-bones reasoning will suffice.

I would hesitate to say, as a general proposition, that the same can be said when the dispute is complex or high-stake, or one in which the parties have invested much effort in marshalling abundant and sophisticated evidence and developing elaborate arguments, even if ultimately they turn out not to be outcome-determinative. In such cases, it seems to me that the tribunal owes it to the parties and their counsel to explain that even those arguments have been duly understood and considered.

This is particularly so in cases where there is a difference of opinion within the tribunal and of awards that are likely to become public, and even more so in investor-State arbitration. Here the addressees of the award are in practical terms not just the parties involved but, in addition perhaps to *amici*, also the public at large, which may well not have a clear understanding of the issues in dispute, and from whose viewpoint a broader perspective on them may be useful. The higher the stakes and implications, the stronger I believe is the case for erring on the side of exhaustiveness.

I am therefore not sure there should necessarily be a sharp dividing line between investor-State arbitration, for which exhaustiveness of the reasoning is almost taken for granted, and commercial arbitration. I think fairly similar considerations can apply to important commercial disputes, particularly those where States or State entities of public interests are involved—although one difference is that investor-State awards normally become public which is less likely for commercial cases, even involving States.

A related question can be the extent to which, in order to give the complete picture and to put the decision in context, the arbitrators may, or even should, refer to matters or arguments on which the parties have not particularly dwelt or have referred to only tangentially or not at all (and which the arbitrators have not raised with them). In principle, this is something the arbitrators should not do, particularly if it involves the risk of straying into controversial or (worse still) policy or political considerations. One could wonder, however, if in some situations the tribunal should at least mention that certain issues have not been raised, were it only to show that it has not missed them. What I instead think the tribunal can do is rely on authorities or theories not mentioned by the parties if they merely add further support to the solution which the arbitrators would in any event reach based on the theories or arguments developed by the parties, and which increase the persuasiveness of the decision. In such a case there should be no risk of the parties being taken by surprise.

Another situation which requires some reflection is the one where the arbitrators' decision may have implications beyond the case at hand. This is obviously the case for investor-State awards, but may also be the case, for example, where the parties are involved in other similar relationships which may equally give rise to disputes or where the decision deals with an issue that may have broader repercussions in a particular industrial sector. Depending on the situation, these considerations may militate in favour of giving extensive reasons or, instead, greater restraint. From a somewhat different perspective, when the dispute is between parties involved in a broader relationship, the reasoning must not contain elements capable of negatively affecting this relationship and should actually, if possible and appropriate in the circumstances, try to facilitate that relationship.

In principle tribunals should refrain from addressing an issue simply because they have invested a lot of work on it, only to realise at one point that it is not really relevant to the flow of the reasoning. They should also avoid an overly scholarly approach. They should likewise refrain from needlessly castigating the parties or the lawyers for what they have said or not said, except perhaps where that is called for in order to explain that certain arguments negatively impacted the efficiency, speed and cost of the proceedings. But here also the arbitrators need to be careful because, depending on the circumstances and issues at stake, the parties may be justified in wanting to raise all possible arguments to support their case even if they end up not to be winning ones, or might have from the beginning appeared to be a long shot.

On the other hand, the tribunal must not succumb to the temptation of taking shortcuts to sidestep difficult issues by failing to give adequate reasons or providing only minimal reasons, perhaps relying on the fact that its reasoning is largely beyond the review of the courts. It is true that courts are very loath to set aside for failure to state reasons, and rightly so because such a review would be fatal. This has just been confirmed by the English High Court in *The Islamic Republic of Pakistan and the National Accountability Bureau v Broadsheet LLC* ([2019] EWHC 1832 (Comm)), which also held (at para. 47) that the standard is the same when a State is a party to the arbitration. I submit, however, that this definitely should not be taken to mean that arbitrators should not go beyond the bare minimum that suffices to avoid setting aside. Providing reasons for their decision is a fundamental part of their job and they should therefore put into it all the efforts and diligence commensurate to the type of dispute and issues before them.

Also for this reason tribunals should not cave in to the pressure of institutions breathing down their backs to issue the award quickly if, in the circumstances, the reasoning needs to be particularly elaborate. This of course does not justify inordinate delays in the issuance of the award.

IV. CONCLUSION

These are admittedly all fairly general considerations that need to be balanced and adapted to each case and that for the most part apply both to investor-State and to commercial arbitration. As I said before, and as is obvious, there is no single way to write an award. A lot depends on the circumstances, and much is a question of style that will depend on the personality of individual arbitrators. The greater or lesser experience and confidence, and reputation, of the arbitrators may also play a role in how they decide to deal with the different issues in the award.

Concretely, arbitrators need to use their broad discretion well and to strike a delicate balance between saying too much and saying too little, always keeping in mind the expectations of all those concerned by the arbitration, as well as the need to render an award capable of withstanding challenges—which may mean saying certain things and not saying other ones. Since they lack the same authority of judges, they should strive to be as exhaustive and convincing as possible.

One thing that definitely must be avoided is a reasoning in which the actual reasoning consists of a few pages sandwiched in between hundreds of pages of recital of procedural history, facts and positions of the parties. This type of award is totally unsatisfactory for the parties and goes against their legitimate expectations. The complaint of excessive length of certain awards, particularly in investor-State cases, may not be due to the length itself, but to the lack of proportion in some of them between the actual reasoning and peripheral material.

A point that would deserve some consideration is whether the content of the award, and in particular the level of detail of the reasoning, could be the subject of discussion between the tribunal and the parties at some, preferably early, stage of the arbitration. It is certainly open to the parties to flag to the tribunal any particular wishes or needs they may have in this respect, so that the matter can be appropriately codified in the terms of reference or appointment or in a procedural order.

A final consideration, to which little attention is devoted, is that in deciding what to write in their award arbitrators should also be particularly attentive to the implications of their reasoning on the *res judicata* effects of the award. These depend in part on the applicable law, the identification of which is itself a very difficult subject. To simplify, there are different conceptions on the *res judicata* of awards, under some of which also the reasoning may have certain preclusive and conclusive effects. Where that may be the case, the arbitrators have to consider with care how broad they want the effects of their decision to be.

As it is the case for so many issues in arbitration, the ultimate solution lies on a judicious exercise of discretion on the part of the arbitrators.

Chapter 6

Reasoning in Arbitral Awards: Why? How?

Control and Sanction under Swiss Law

by Teresa Giovannini B.*

I. INTRODUCTION

The 2013 Swiss Arbitration Association (ASA) Annual Conference was entitled "Inside the Black Box: How Arbitral Tribunals operate and Reach their Decisions". Dr Bernhard Berger, a renowned expert in the field, introduced the theme as follows:

> (...) from the parties' perspective, you know the arguments and motions put forward in the proceedings, that is the input; you can see the result in the form of the dispositive section of the award, that is the output; and you can try to understand the reasons given for the decision in the award, that will be the transfer element. All the rest that may have happened in the deliberations remains undisclosed and undiscovered: for example, is there a relatively mild decision on the quantum of damages as a bargaining chip for the unanimous affirmation of liability?[1]

This question raises that of the reasoning of the award: how extensive and/or complete must it be for the process to be fully comprehensible and thus legitimate to the parties and in particular to the losing party?

The requirement that, unless otherwise agreed by the parties, the award "shall state the reasons upon which it is based" is a widely recognized principle in international arbitration. It is expressly formulated in the UNCITRAL Model Law on International Commercial Arbitration (UNCITRAL Model Law)[2] and in the vast majority of national laws, be they Model Law inspired[3] or not[4]. The principle is likewise expressed in almost all international arbitration rules[5].

The first question that arises in this respect is straightforward: "why" is this requirement deemed to be so important as to be expressed everywhere (*infra*, section II)?

In the absence of any legal or regulatory directions as to the content of the legal or regulatory duty to provide reasons for the award, the second question that inevitably arises is clearly "how" can the requirement be met in a way that satisfies the principles which form the basis of the requirement and thus the user (*infra*, section III)?

The last question that requires our attention is the court's approach which, in certain cases, may sanction to an unsatisfactory reasoning. This question will be addressed, regarding in particular the Swiss Supreme Court's jurisprudence (*infra*,section IV).

* Founding Partner, LALIVE; Member of the ICC International Court of Arbitration; Council Member, ICC Institute of World Business Law

II. REASONING IN ARBITRATION: WHY?

II.A. As Source of Legitimacy of the Decision[6]

Immanuel Kant (Germany, 1724-1804), one of the greatest philosophers of all times, was the first to apply to philosophy the idea of astronomer Nicolas Copernic that the Earth was not the centre of the universe (as believed in those times), but rather that the sun was at the centre while the Earth moved around it. This concept entirely changed the way of thinking[7]: the centre of the human world was no longer the egocentric "I" but rather my relation to "You" so as "to treat humanity, whether in thine own person or in that of any other, in every case as an end, never as means only."[8] For Kant, we treat people as an end whenever our actions towards them reflect their inherent value[9].

The concept is mirrored in the conclusion reached at the outcome of the Alexandrine Day dedicated to Philippe Fouchard on 28 April 2005: the economic and the business world cannot survive without ethics and the survival of capitalism and liberalism is subject to the condition that the human being is not forgotten.

Jürgen Habermas, another renowned philosopher (Germany, 1929-), follows Kant's way of thinking in putting forward the principle of publicity, namely the requirement of a critical and public use of the reason. This principle comes within the broader frame of the deliberative democracy. For the German philosopher, a decision is legitimate only insofar as it results from a legitimate process called "deliberative process" consisting in the manner in which the problems have been formulated and the way the solutions have been evaluated being made public. This principle is said by Kant to be a source of lawfulness against despotism. It stands up against the decision-maker model put forward by Jean-Jacques Rousseau that states that the source of the decision is sufficient for guaranteeing its legitimacy.[10]

The concept was precisely addressed by the Swedish Supreme Court in a decision from 2009:

> [a] description of sufficient reasoning in an arbitration award constitutes a guarantee of legal certainty, since it forces the arbitral tribunal to analyse the legal issues and the evidence.[11]

As a result, I would dare to reformulate the question put to this panel in wondering *what are the users entitled to*?

II.B. Reasoning as evidence of comprehension

As suggested above, the first objective for the decision maker would be the entities/individuals concerned—the parties—to be considered and seen to be considered as an end so that to reflect their inherent value. Such an objective is inherent to the process of evaluation the addressee of the decision is legitimately entitled to and entitled to have knowledge of.

In that regard, and as put by the renowned contemporary French Philosopher Edgar Morin, "information does not provide understanding". When we really attempt to understand each other, again always according to Morin, there are three types of comprehension:

(i) The "objective comprehension", namely the understanding of the explanation provided. This type of comprehension assembles data and objective information concerning a person, a behaviour or a situation;

(ii) The "subjective comprehension", "that is from subject to subject, from person to person". This comprehension is more emotional, enabling us to understand another person's motivations and feelings;

(iii) The "complex comprehension", which includes both objective and subjective comprehension. This complex comprehension tends to avoid reducing a person to one single trait or see him/her, or it if it is a group, in only one light. It tends to encompass the various dimensions of the person or entity and the multiplicity of his/her/its various roles.[12]

Morin's approach can easily be transposed into the international business arena in general and the resolution of international disputes in particular as a practical tool to prevent parties' dissatisfaction with the way decisions are drafted and communicated.

Inspiration can be drawn in this respect from the contents of judgments issued by different judicial bodies. For example, the Swiss Federal Tribunal generally sets out in the first place the reasons why the recourse must fail or succeed. The Federal Tribunal thereafter addresses all the other defences addressed by the parties in explaining how and why such defences cannot alter the decision made. This is precisely the methodology suggested by Morin in that it includes a proper and independent reasoning on (all) the arguments a party has considered as relevant for its case despite the fact that these very same arguments were not held as such for the decision maker.

II.C. Reasoning as Evidence of the Abeyance to the Parties Fundamental Right to Due Process

As put by the then deputy president of the UK Supreme Court, Lord Hope of Craighead, in an (unpublished) lecture on legal reasoning:[13]

> Clear reasoning and analysis are basic requirements in judicial decisions and an important aspect of the article 6 *[of the European Convention on Human Rights]* right to a fair trial.
>
> The reader, whoever he or she is, should be able to understand what led us to the conclusions that we have reached.
>
> [The judgment] has to satisfy the rule of law that says that the litigant has a right to know why he has won or lost his case.
>
> The key is to think of your audience and to imagine yourself having to justify your reasoning to it face to face. Although you are setting out your conclusions on paper, the techniques are those that you might want to use if you were having to debate the issue orally. There is no need to go on at length if the point can be made quite simply. But there are some borderline cases where it is worth making the effort to reason the arguments out point by point.

II.D. Reasoning as a Tool Necessary for Court Scrutiny

Last but not least, reasoning is generally the only means a court disposes of to verify the award compliance with the basic principles of validity and enforceability under the UNCITRAL Model Law[14] and the 1958 Convention on the Recognition and Enforcement of Foreign Arbitral Awards (New York Convention)[15], in particular of the parties' right to be heard and the non-violation of public policy principles.

III. REASONING IN ARBITRATION: HOW?

Following the principle of publicity set forth by the German philosopher Habermas, what may have happened in the deliberations should be made known to the parties. This is precisely what the reasoning should serve to do, namely, to communicate to the parties the manner in which the problems have been formulated and the way the solutions have been evaluated by the tribunal.

Put differently, it is the author's view that the award can be held as legitimate by the parties to the extent that they can be satisfied that the tribunal has addressed all the problems they hold as relevant to the decision to make, and this, in a full and comprehensive way.

This approach puts the focus on the decision-making process and the way it could be made visible to the parties.

The parties' views in response to the Arbitral Tribunal identifying as soon as possible in the proceedings both the key questions to be decided and the methodology by which the decisions must be arrived at can constitute a very efficient tool to such an end.[16] Such a consultation process can permit the parties to make sure their concerns are being considered and to comment as the case may be on the methodology that will be followed to resolve them.

Another component of the decision-making process that can constitute an important indication on the tribunal's approach to the issues at stake consists in the document production process, or more broadly put, the issue of the burden and weighing of the evidence. More often than not, this issue is simply referred to in the terms of reference or in the first procedural order by reference to existing rules, such as the so-called IBA Rules[17] or the Prague Rules,[18] without further ado. Here again, a real debate at the outset of the proceedings can considerably enhance the transparency of the way the evidence will be considered and weighed by the tribunal, possibly leading to a general agreement between the protagonists. Such a debate would also present the advantage of having the rules of the game clearly established, which, as practice shows, is not so obvious (e.g. obligation, or lack of obligation, to produce documents adverse to one's position).

To sum up, I believe that a decision will be deemed legitimate to the parties concerned, if the reasoning is the express outcome of deliberations led with as much transparency as possible. In the paragraphs above I have suggested some tools to that end; there surely exist others.

IV. CONTROL AND SANCTION OF THE TRIBUNAL'S REASONING

IV.A. Introduction

The generally recognized legal duty to provide reasons for the award finds support in particular in the control exercised by the courts of the validity of the award and/or of its recognition and enforcement.

The chapter that follows will specifically concentrate on the control exercised by the Swiss Supreme Court as an illustration of one of the modern legislations and approaches to the security of a valid and enforceable award.

IV.B. The Requirement of Reasons

The requirement for awards to be supported by reasoning is expressed in Article 189.2 of the Swiss Private International Law Act (PILA) that reads as follows:

> The arbitral award shall be rendered in conformity with the rules of procedure and in the form agreed upon by the parties.
>
> In the absence of such an agreement, the arbitral award shall be made by a majority, or, in the absence of a majority, by the chairman alone. The award shall be in writing, supported by reasons, dated and signed. The signature of the chairman is sufficient.[19]

This legal provision calls for three major considerations:

(i) First, the obligation to provide reasons—as it is the case for state courts—is restricted to allowing a party to understand the main reasons supporting the decision and to assess the possibilities of appeal.[20]

(ii) Secondly, the obligation only applies to awards, namely decisions which, for procedural or substantive reasons, end the arbitral proceedings in respect of all (final awards) or part (partial awards) of the claims and are subject to annulment proceedings.[21] The qualification of a decision as an award depends on its content rather than on its formal designation by the arbitral tribunal. Therefore, a "procedural order" which rules on substantive issues needs to be motivated as per Article 189 PILA;[22] similarly, an "order" that closes the proceedings has to be considered as an award with the legal requirement of an explicit motivation.[23] By contrast, orders on provisional measures which can be lifted or modified at any time during the proceedings do not fall under the scope of application of the legal provision mentioned and therefore would not be subject as a matter of principle to the requirement of reasoning.[24]

(iii) Thirdly, the parties are entitled to waive the requirement of the reasoning in the award any time during the proceedings and after the notification of the dispositive part of an award.[25] The waiver may also occur by conclusive acts.[26]

Moreover, it has to be stressed that the waiver to the reasoning does not amount to a waiver of the possibility to apply for the setting aside of the award,[27] even though such a waiver impairs significantly the chances for a party to have an award annulled.[28] Similarly, a waiver does not impair the parties' right to have the award enforced.[29]

IV.C. The Control

IV.C.1. The Grounds for Annulment under Swiss Law

Article 190.2 PILA sets forth the list of the grounds for annulment of international awards as follows:

The award may only be annulled:

a) if the sole arbitrator was not properly appointed or if the arbitral tribunal was not properly constituted;

b) if the arbitral tribunal wrongly accepted or declined jurisdiction;

c) if the arbitral tribunal's decision went beyond the claims submitted to it, or failed to decide one of the items of the claim;

d) if the principle of equal treatment of the parties or the right of the parties to be heard was violated;

e) if the award is incompatible with public policy.

The Supreme Court's jurisprudence has constantly affirmed in the first place that given the lack of, or insufficient reasoning not being included in the exhaustive list of grounds under Article 190.2 PILA, it cannot therefore *per se* constitute a ground for annulment of the award.[30]

The Supreme Court has also constantly held that the lack of reasoning is not "in and of itself" incompatible with public policy[31] including in the context of recognition and enforcement of awards.[32] Even an intrinsic inconsistency in the reasons of the award or a contradiction between the reasons and the dispositive is not covered by the concept of public policy under Article 190.2 PILA.[33]

The lack of reasoning has however been found to be relevant in the context of the parties' right to be heard under Article 190.2(d) PILA which requires in particular that the arbitral tribunal, while under no obligation to provide an express and reasoned decision on a given request,[34] is under a minimum duty to examine and dispose of the issues that are both material and relevant to the outcome of the case. This duty is violated when, by oversight or misunderstanding, the arbitral tribunal fails to consider factual allegations, arguments, evidence and offers of evidence presented by a party and which are important for the decision to be rendered.[35]

The lack of reasoning can, however, be overcome by the tribunal itself which—under Swiss law—is entitled to submit a determination in response to the recourse, by either explaining that the issue was considered as not decisive or that the argument was implicitly dismissed.[36]

Finally, as rightly emphasised by the Swiss Supreme Court, lack of (or by extension insufficient) reasoning is susceptible to "considerably reduce the chances of success of a recourse".[37]

V. CONCLUSION

It is this author's conviction that what the parties need (the winner also wants to understand the reasons for its victory that can have an important impact on the business at stake) is what Dr Berger mentioned at the outset of the ASA Conference: information on the decision-making process, more precisely on the manner in which the problems and the solutions have been identified and evaluated.

The only practical response to this concern is, in my view, in the deliberative process being made public as set forth by Habermas, precisely having the parties participate as much as feasibly possible in the setting up of the mechanism itself and the way it will be run. Put differently, the parties should be involved in identifying, on the one hand, the issues that must be considered to ensure both objective and subjective comprehension and, on the other hand, the methodology (including on the weighing of evidence) that will be followed by the tribunal.

The reasoning of the award would then just mirror the results reached by applying a methodology shared with, or at least known to, the parties beforehand.

This is what in my opinion the users are entitled to.

NOTES

1. Berger, Bernhard, "The Legal Framework: Rights and Obligations of the Arbitrators in the Deliberations", in *Berger, Bernhard and Schneider, Michael E.* (eds.), "Inside the Black Box; How Arbitral Tribunals Operate and Reach their Decisions", *ASA Special Series No. 42* (2014), p. 7.
2. UNCITRAL Model Law, Article 31.2.
3. e.g., in Switzerland, Swiss Private International Law Act, Article 189.2.
4. e.g., in China, Arbitration Law of the People's Republic of China, Article 54.
5. e.g., ICC Rules, Article 32.2; LCIA Rules, Article 26.2.
6. The chapter that follows is partly inspired from the author's speech delivered at the Annual Meeting of the American Arbitration Association's Board of Directors in Montreal on 5 May 2011, published as Giovannini, Teresa, "Philosophy Can Help Tribunals Draft Awards that Parties Will Accept as Legitimate", International Arbitration, May/July 2011, p. 78 et seq.
7. *13 Encyclopaedia Universalis*, p. 260.
8. id, p. 265.
9. Internet Encyclopedia of Philosophy, Ethics, available at: https://www.iep.utm.edu/ethics/.
10. Wikipedia, Jürgen Habermas, available at: https://fr.wikipedia.org/wiki/J%C3%BCrgen_Habermas.
11. Swedish Supreme Court, *Soyak v Hochtief*, NJA 2009, p. 128, 31 March 2009, cited in Hope, James and Rosengren, Mattias, "A call for Reason", 16 August 2013, Commercial Dispute Resolution, available at: https://www.cdr-news.com/categories/arbitration-and-adr/a-call-for-reason.
12. Address by Edgar Morin, *Round Table: Dialogue Among Civilizations*, United Nations, New York, 5 September 2000, Provisional verbatim transcription, available at: www.unesco.org/dialogue/en/morin2.hm.
13. Lord Hope of Craighead, unpublished lecture on legal reasoning, delivered to the Judicial Studies Committee Seminar on 14 November 2011, quoted Hope, James and Rosengren, Mattias, *op. cit. supra*, footnote 12.
14. See UNCITRAL Model Law, Articles 34 and 36.
15. New York Convention, Article V.
16. Bunni, Nael G., "Personal Views on How Arbitral Tribunals Operate and Reach Their Decisions", *in Berger, Bernhard and Schneider, Michael E. (eds.), op. cit. supra*, footnote 2, p. 123.
17. IBA Rules on the Taking of Evidence in International Arbitration, Adopted by a resolution of the IBA Council on 29 May 2010.
18. Rules on the Efficient Conduct of Proceedings in International Arbitration (Prague Rules) (2018).
19. PILA, Article 189.
20. Poudret, Jean-François and Besson, Sébastien, "Comparative Law of International Arbitration" (2007), para. 749.
21. See Molina, Martin, "Commentary on Chapter 12 PILA, Article 189", in Arroyo, Manuel (ed.), *Arbitration in Switzerland: The Practitioner's Guide* (2018), p. 243, para. 4, with reference to Lalive, Pierre, Poudret, Jean-François and Reymond, Claude, "Le droit de l'arbitrage interne et international en Suisse" (1989), paras 1-2 at Art.189, and paras 3-4 at Art. 188; Heini, Anton, in Girsberger, Daniel et al. (eds.), *Zürcher Kommentar zum IPRG* (2004), paras 3-4 at Art. 189; and Wirth, Markus, in Honsell, Heinrich et al. (eds.), *Basler Kommentar Internationales Privatrecht* (2013), paras 2-4 at Art. 189.
22. Molina, Martin, *op. cit. supra*, footnote 22, p. 244, para. 8.

23. SFT 4A_600/2008 of 20 February 2009, E. 2.3:

    (...) pour juger de la recevabilité du recours, ce qui est déterminant n'est pas la dénomination du prononcé entrepris, mais le contenu de celui-ci. De ce point de vue, il n'est pas douteux que, dans sa décision, le TAS ne s'est pas borné à fixer la suite de la procédure. Il y constate que l'avance de frais requise n'a pas été faite dans le délai fixé à cet effet et en tire la conséquence que prévoit l'art. R64.2 du Code, c'est-à-dire la fiction irréfragable du retrait de l'appel. Son prononcé s'apparente à une décision d'irrecevabilité qui clôt l'affaire pour un motif tiré des règles de la procedure.

    In free translation: "(...) in order to assess the admissibility of the appeal, what is decisive is not the name of the pronouncement, but its content. From this point of view, there is no doubt that in its decision the CAS did not limit itself to fixing the rest of the proceedings. It finds that the advance of costs was not paid within the time fixed for this purpose and draws the consequence provided for in art. R64.2 of the Code, that is, the irrevocable withdrawal of the appeal. Its pronouncement is similar to a decision of inadmissibility which closes the case for a procedural reason."
24. Molina, Martin, *op. cit. supra*, footnote 22, p. 243, para. 7.
25. Berger, Bernhard and Kellerhals, Franz, "International and Domestic Arbitration in Switzerland" (2015), para. 1543 and fn 8.
26. SFT 5P.315/2003 BGE 130 III 125 of 9 December 2009, E. 2.2.
27. A possibility that is expressly contemplated by Article 190(1) PILA as follows:

    [i]f none of the parties have their domicile, their habitual residence, or a business establishment in Switzerland, they may, by an express statement in the arbitration agreement or by a subsequent written agreement, waive fully the action for annulment or they may limit it to one or several of the grounds listed in Art. 190(2).
28. SFT 4A_198/2012 of 14 December 2012 E.2.2.
29. id.
30. Molina, Martin, *op. cit. supra*, footnote 22, p. 772, para. 20. See SFT 5P.315/2003 BGE 130 III 125 of 9 December 2009, E. 2.2.; and SFT 4P.26/2005 of 23 March 2005, E.3.2.
31. Berger, Bernhard and Kellerhals, Franz, *op. cit. supra*, footnote 26, para. 1745, with reference to 4P.17/1990 BGE 116 II 373 of 21 August 1990, E.7b.
32. Berger, Bernhard and Kellerhals, Franz, *op. cit. supra*, footnote 26, para. 1745 with reference to BGE 101 IA 521 of 12 December 1975, E.4.
33. See Berger, Bernhard and Kellerhals, Franz, *op. cit. supra*, footnote 26, para. 1788, with reference to SFT 4P.282/2001 BGE 128 III 191 of 3 April 2002, E.6b; SFT 4A_612/2009 of 10 February 2010 E.6.2.2.; SFT 4A_464/2009 of 15 February 2010, E.5.1, holding that the objection based on intrinsic inconsistency of the reasons of an award does not fall under the definition of substantive public policy in the meaning of Article 190.2(e); and 4_A 386/2010 of 3 January 2011, E.8.3.1
34. See, e.g., SFT 4P.26/2005 of 23 March 2005, E.3.2: "une autorité ne viole pas le droit d'être entendu si elle n'examine pas des questions qu'elle n'estime pas décisives, à bon droit, pour la solution du cas", in free translation: "an authority does not violate the right to be heard if it does not consider issues that it does not deem decisive, rightly, for the solution of the case"; and SFT 4A_468/2007 BGE 134 III 186 of 22 January 2008 E.6., 6.1. and 6.2.
35. See SFT 4A_46/2011 of 16 May 2011, E.4.3.1: annulment of the award as a consequence of an arbitral tribunal's failure to address the statute of limitation as argued by the aggrieved party for the first time in the post-hearing brief; and SFT 4.A 460/2013 of 4 February 2014, E.3.3: annulment of the award as a consequence of an arbitral tribunal's failure to consider the contractual exclusion of liability for certain damages, which was expressly invoked in the arbitration. See Berger, Bernhard and Kellerhals, Franz, *op. cit. supra*, footnote 26, para. 1748.
36. See Molina, Martin, *op. cit. supra*, footnote 22, p. 772, para. 21, with reference to SFT 4A_46/2011 of 16 May 2011, E.4.3.1 and others.
37. SFT 4A_198/2012 of 14 December 2012, E.2.2, free translation from French original.

Chapter 7
Reasoning in Arbitration: What Do Users Want or Need?

by Giuditta Cordero-Moss*

I. INTRODUCTION

Traditionally, the reasoning of awards rendered in international commercial disputes is expected to meet a standard that is sufficient to explain the basis upon which the tribunal decided. The purpose is usually to convince the parties that the decision is sound. Another purpose is to make sure that the award resists any scrutiny by the courts, either if the validity of the award is challenged or in case of enforcement. Increasingly, however, the reasoning of international arbitral awards is expected to meet further criteria that are not necessarily compatible with each other.

On the one hand, the significant attention devoted in the international arbitration community to investment arbitration, and particularly the regular publication and analysis of most arbitral awards that are rendered in investment disputes, seems to be exercising a force of attraction on the style in which commercial awards are written. Due to the presence of general interests in investment disputes, and certainly also due to the publicity that surrounds most investment awards, such investment awards tend to contain lengthy and thorough reasons. Investment awards are written with the awareness that they are going to be studied and discussed in the legal community, and used as precedents. Therefore, investment tribunals devote considerable attention to the compilation of reasons that not only solve the dispute at hand but may also be useful to the development of the law. This also contributes to the proliferation of dissenting opinions. Commercial awards, on the contrary, are traditionally confidential and not meant to be perused by anyone else but the parties. However, the calls for transparency are increasingly affecting commercial arbitration as well, and the publication of commercial awards, albeit not as systematic as it is the case for investment awards, is considerably more widespread than in the past. The prospects that the award will be analysed in the legal community is an incitement to write extensive reasoning that may have general interest and increase the possibility for the award to be used as a precedent.

On the other hand, the growing desire to enhance the efficiency of arbitral proceedings seems to suggest that even the need that awards state reasons is questioned. Various forms of expedited arbitration are being developed, and in some instances the reasoning is one of the features deemed dispensable for the sake of enhancing efficiency.

Professor, Department for Private Law, University of Oslo

In summary, the reasoning in commercial arbitral awards is under a double and inconsistent pressure: on the one hand, an expansive pressure aiming at making awards with general relevance and potential of being used as precedent; on the other hand, a restrictive pressure aiming at enhancing efficiency.

In evaluating how to state the reasons of an award, in my opinion, one should not lose sight of the legal constraints that may affect the validity and enforceability of the award. Court control on the validity of awards and court assistance to enforce awards represent an indispensable legal framework, and awards should state reasons to the extent that reasons are required to permit the exercise of court control. Anything less is not advisable, because it leads to rendering awards that potentially may be set aside or refused enforcement. Anything more is not necessary for the purpose of ensuring the validity and enforceability of an award. It is disputable whether it is useful, for the purpose of ensuring the credibility of arbitration, to exceed the standard for reasons required for passing court scrutiny: arguably, an award with reasons that are sufficient to meet the requirements for court control should be sufficient to satisfy the standard for credibility that is expected of a dispute resolution method.

In this paper, I will go through the requirements that awards have to meet in order to resist court scrutiny, and I will make some considerations on what is needed and what is advisable or not advisable in terms of reasoning.

II. REASONING OF THE AWARD AND COURT CONTROL

A court who controls the validity or the enforceability of an award derives its jurisdiction from the applicable law. In case of challenge to the award's validity, the applicable law is the arbitration law prevailing at the place of arbitration. In case of the award's enforcement, the applicable law is, in the 159 countries having ratified it, [1] the New York Convention. [2]

National arbitration law differs from country to country, therefore the court's jurisdiction in case of challenge to the award's validity needs to be analysed on the basis of the national law that is applicable in the specific case. For the sake of simplicity, however, we will assume here that the national arbitration law corresponds to the 1985 UNCITRAL Model Law on International Commercial Arbitration (revised in 2006),[3] as it does, more or less literally, in the 80 countries that are considered to be "Model Law countries".[4]

As the court's powers, to the extent that is relevant here, are equivalent in the New York Convention and in the Model Law,[5] the analysis can be made without distinguishing between court control carried out in connection with challenge to the award's validity and court control carried out in connection with enforcement of the award. However, it should be emphasised that, if the law applicable in a specific case does not belong to a Model Law country, or if it implements the Model Law with some discrepancies from the original, it will be necessary to verify whether the law applicable to annulment has diverging regulation.

The applicable provisions make it clear that court control is not meant to be an appeal. Court control is not the same as a review of the award on the merits, neither in respect of the assessment of facts nor in respect of the application of law. The direct consequence of this limitation of court control is that an award is final and binding, even if it contains errors of fact or errors of law. This is the basis upon which the system of arbitration, as we know it today, rests: international conventions, national laws, courts of law, legal doctrine and practitioners support the aim that arbitration is to be an effective and efficient means of dispute resolution. To achieve this aim, they widely recognise that awards must be final and binding. Effectiveness and efficiency of arbitration are important principles of arbitration law, and at the origin of the widespread arbitration-friendly attitude that has characterised legislation and case law in the past decades. This seems to suggest that the controlling court shall not be concerned with the award's reasons: even if the reasons show that the arbitral tribunal got the facts or the law wrongly, the court does not have the authority to react.

However, as will be seen below, the award's reasons may be useful or even necessary in the context of court control. The provisions regulating court control on arbitral awards represent the limit of tolerance that legal systems have in respect of arbitral awards. As seen above, an award containing errors of fact or errors of law shall be confirmed as valid and shall be enforced.

However, an award rendered by an arbitral tribunal whose jurisdiction did not rest on a valid and binding arbitration agreement is not valid (article 34(2)(a)(i) of the Model Law) and not enforceable (article 36(1)(a)(i) of the Model Law and article V(1)(a) of the New York Convention); an award rendered as a result of a proceeding that did not give each of the parties the possibility to present its case is not valid (article 34(2)(a)(ii) of the Model Law) and not enforceable (article 36(1)(a)(ii) of the Model Law and article V(1)(b) of the New York Convention); an award rendered in excess of the jurisdiction granted on the arbitral tribunal is not valid (article 34(2)(a)(iii) of the Model Law) and not enforceable (article 36(1)(a)(iii) of the Model Law and article V(1)(c) of the New York Convention); an award rendered by an arbitral tribunal that was not constituted in accordance with the parties' agreement or the applicable law, or as a result of proceedings that did not comply with the parties' agreement or the applicable procedural rules is not valid (article 34(2)(a)(iv) of the Model Law) and not enforceable (article 36(1)(a)(iv) of the Model Law and article V(1)(d) of the New York Convention); an award rendered on a non-arbitrable subject-matter is not valid (article 34(2)(b)(i) of the Model Law) and not enforceable (article 36(1)(b)(i) of the Model Law and article V(2)(a) of the New York Convention); an award infringing fundamental principles (public policy) is not valid (article 34(2)(b)(ii) of the Model Law) and not enforceable (article 36(1)(b)(ii) of the Model Law and article V(2)(b) of the New York Convention).

There is a certain tension between the principle that court control is not a review of the award on the merits, on one hand, and the courts' power to set aside an award or refuse its enforcement, on the other hand.

This becomes clear particularly when the court exercises control on a matter that already has been considered by the arbitral tribunal. As was seen above, there is an exhaustive list of issues the court may evaluate: whether the arbitration agreement was valid or the parties had legal capacity to enter into it, whether the principle of due process was respected, whether the tribunal's constitution or procedure was in accordance with the parties' will and the applicable rules, whether the tribunal exceeded its power, whether the object of the dispute was arbitrable and whether the award infringes public policy. If the tribunal has not considered the matter at all, the tension does not become evident: the court exercises its power to determine these issues, and this does not interfere with an evaluation already made by the tribunal. It may interfere with the award if the outcome is that the award is set aside or not enforced. However, it does not interfere with the tribunal's evaluation of the particular issues regarding the validity of the arbitration agreement, the parties' legal capacity, etc., because the tribunal has not evaluated these issues.

All the above-mentioned issues underlying the courts' power to control arbitral awards may, however, conceivably have been already evaluated by the arbitral tribunal. The tribunal may have considered whether the arbitration agreement met the applicable form requirements or whether a party had legal capacity to enter into it, and it may have concluded in the affirmative, thus proceeding to solving the dispute in the merits and rendering an award. Yet the courts may have a different opinion of the same issues and may conclude that the award shall be set aside or refused enforcement. The same reasoning may be made in respect of the other grounds for setting aside or refusing enforcement: the tribunal may have considered its constitution, the procedure followed under the dispute, the scope of its power, the arbitrability of the disputed object, or the conformity of the award with fundamental principles; the tribunal may have concluded that there were no violations. Yet the court may have a different opinion, and it may exercise its power to set aside the award or refuse its enforcement.

The above-mentioned tension between the principle of the award's finality and court control becomes, therefore, particularly evident in case of concurrent, and diverging, evaluations of the same issue carried out by the tribunal and by the court. Is the court reviewing the arbitral tribunal's evaluation of these issues? This is at odds with the principle of no review of the award in the merits. Is the court independently carrying out its own examination of these issues? This is compatible with the court's power to exercise control on the award. The court's activity is the same in both situations, but the description of this activity is different and leads to different results. Where does the border go between these two conflicting descriptions of the same court activity? And which role do the reasons stated in the award play?

From the foregoing it appears that the award's reasons are necessary to determine whether the arbitral tribunal has examined an issue. If the matter was not addressed in the award, and if it falls within the above-mentioned grounds for annulling or refusing enforcement, the court will independently consider the matter and decide the issue. The reasons of the award, therefore, are necessary to prevent annulment of refusal of enforcement on the basis that the arbitral tribunal did not consider issues such as the validity of the arbitration agreement, the legal capacity of the parties, the respect of due process, the regulatory of the procedure or of the constitution of the arbitral tribunal, the scope of power conferred on the arbitral tribunal by the parties, the arbitrability of the dispute or the compatibility of the award with public policy. That the arbitral tribunal did not evaluate these issues is not, in itself, a ground for annulling the award or refusing its enforcement, but the court will have no basis upon which to develop its independent evaluation of these issues. If the court, on the basis of its evaluation, determines that the award is not in compliance with the relevant criteria, it will set aside the award or refuse its enforcement.

But what happens if the arbitral tribunal has considered these issues, has written a reasoned award that explains the arbitral tribunal's views thereon, and the court disagrees with the award's reasoning?

The matter has been perhaps mostly discussed in connection with two of the above-mentioned issues: whether the arbitral tribunal has jurisdiction to hear the dispute (particularly in connection with whether there is a valid and binding arbitration agreement), and whether the award violates public policy. There seems to be an inconsistency in the answer to the question, depending on the context in which it arises. This, and the significance that it has for the reasons of the award, will be addressed in sections IV. and V. below.

The controlling court does not necessarily direct its attention to the award's reasons: with the exception of the minimalist doctrine relating to the public policy rule, that will be discussed in section V. below, the court forms its own opinion of whether the award meets the above-mentioned criteria for validity and enforceability. In theory, therefore, a court does not need to read the award's reasons. However, as will be seen in section VI., knowing the reasoning upon which the tribunal's decision was based is necessary when the court has to decide whether the tribunal exceeded its power. The award's reasons play a role also in respect of the remaining criteria for validity and enforceability, discussed in sections IV., VII. and VIII. below, as well as the maximalist doctrine relating to the public policy rule, that will be discussed in section V. The award's reasons provide a useful insight into the factual elements, the legal sources and the arguments that led to the decision. If the award did not state any reasons, it is not certain that the court would have in front of it all elements useful to make its own determination of the validity and enforceability of the award. Therefore, the award's reasons contribute to a sound court control by permitting the court to examine the elements that were considered by the arbitral tribunal.

III. REASONING OF THE AWARD AND CREDIBILITY OF ARBITRATION

In addition to being necessary or useful to the exercise of court control, the reasons of the award have an important function in respect of the credibility of arbitration as a mechanism for settling disputes.

As known, arbitration is often praised for being an autonomous dispute resolution mechanism that is based on the parties' will, that is only minimally subject to national laws, and only exceptionally subject to court control. This suggests that it is completely up to the parties or the tribunal to decide whether and to what extent to write reasons, as long as the (few) requirements for validity and enforceability are met. This is confirmed by the circumstance that under some sources, such as the Model Law, parties may agree that the award shall not have reasons. As will be seen in section IX. below, however, this possibility creates some difficulties when the lack of reasons prevents a proper court control.

Quite irrespective of the importance of the award's reasons for the exercise of court control, it is my opinion that permitting an award to be without reasons may affirm the autonomy of arbitration in the specific case, but in the long run it creates the risk that arbitration loses its effectiveness. An award without reasons is meant to create legal effects for the parties and must be enforced by the courts, but at the same time gives no basis to determine whether the decision was sound or arbitrary. By not stating reasons, the tribunal does not explain the legal basis for its order, the evidence upon which it has reached its conclusion, etc. Courts are expected to nevertheless recognise and enforce the decision, although they are not capable of verifying the basis upon which the decision was taken. While it is true that the effectiveness of arbitration requires that courts do not review the merits of the award, depriving the award of the basic elements to ensure a minimum of transparency seems to be an unnecessary statement of autonomy. As long as arbitration is meant as a way of solving disputes on legal terms, it should comply with the essence of an adjudicative system, which requires that the basis for the decision is known or understandable.[6] It has been suggested that, if the parties wish to avoid that the arbitral tribunal be constrained by legal rules, including the necessity to write reasons for the purpose of safeguarding the quality of the adjudication process, they may instruct the tribunal to decide *ex aequo et bono*.[7]

By permitting that awards have the legal effects of a court decision, but without having to comply with the most basic notions of the adjudication process, the risk is that the trust in the arbitration system will be eroded, and that this leads courts being more restrictive in determining which disputes may be subject to arbitration.

As known, lack of arbitrability is a ground for setting aside an award and for refusing its enforcement; and what is arbitrable is determined by the courts under their national law. Even the New York Convention specifies, in article V (2) (a), that arbitrability is determined under the court's law. Therefore, it is relatively easy for a court to restrict the scope of what is arbitrable—easier than if arbitrability was a category defined autonomously on an international level.

A parallel could be drawn with the relationship between the possibility to exercise court control and the scope of arbitrability. Elsewhere[8] I have pointed out that restricting the scope of court control creates the risk of reducing the scope of arbitrability. The close link between court control and arbitrability is apparent in some opinions by the CJEU Advocate General ("AG"). In CDC, [9] AG Jääskinen argued for restricting arbitrability of matters relating to competition law, because arbitration, that is not subject to the competence of the CJEU, does not ensure a uniform application of EU law. Similarly, in Genentech,[10] AG Wathelet argued against the minimalist approach to court control. As will be discussed in section V. below, according to the minimalist approach, courts owe deference to the tribunal's evaluation and may not independently verify the compatibility of the award with public policy. In *Achmea*,[11] AG Wathelet accepted the arbitrability of disputes relating to EU law, but on the assumption that courts exercise control on the awards according to the maximalist theory.

In its final judgments on the former two cases, the CJEU ignored the matter. The latter mentioned case, *Achmea*, was based on a referral by the German Supreme Court (BGH) [12] relating to the annulment proceeding of an investment award.[13] One of the invoked annulment grounds was that the award was null because the dispute was not arbitrable: as arbitral tribunals are not bound by the EU duty to apply EU law in a uniform way, the effective application of EU law would be endangered if the dispute had been arbitrable. This line of thought resembled the situation prior to the seminal US case Mitsubishi.[14] Prior to Mitsubishi, US courts excluded arbitrability whenever the issues in dispute assumed the accurate application of norms reflecting important policies, such as competition law. In Mitsubishi, the court affirmed that disputes regarding competition law may be subject to arbitration, as long as the court has the possibility to exercise control on the award (the so-called "second look doctrine"). The Mitsubishi doctrine has informed an era of ever increasing room for arbitrability, both in the USA and in Europe. In *Achmea*, the BGH requested the CJEU to confirm that there is no basis to restrict the scope of arbitrability, as long as the courts may control the award's compatibility with fundamental principles of the forum. Thus, the BGH embraced the second look doctrine introduced by Mitsubishi and endorsed the maximalist theory. AG Wathelet[15] concurred with this line of thought. The CJEU,[16] however, did not accept this approach, and concluded that investment disputes are not arbitrable.[17] However, the CJEU distinguished between investment disputes and commercial disputes, and specified that its conclusion did not apply to commercial disputes. Also this time, therefore, for commercial arbitration the CJEU did not clarify the extent of court control that it expects for it to permit arbitrability of matters related to EU law. The CJEU, however, seemed to indirectly endorse, as an obiter dictum, the AG's assumption that, in controlling commercial arbitral awards, courts should follow the maximalist approach. As I have explained elsewhere,[18] however, the distinction made by the CJEU between investment and commercial arbitration is not convincing. There may be, therefore, reasons to fear that the CJEU turns towards a restrictive approach to arbitrability also in respect of commercial arbitration.

This would confirm a disturbing trend that can be detected in national courts. Courts in EU states such as Austria,[19] Belgium,[20] Germany[21] and England,[22] denied the arbitrability[23] of disputes regarding contracts of commercial agency. EU agency law is deemed to be necessary for the achievement of the internal market. Hence, some courts have affirmed that disputes concerning commercial agency should be decided by courts of EU member states: choosing a court outside the EU, or choosing arbitration, may endanger the effective enforcement of EU law. This shows that domestic courts in a variety of EU member states are assuming a restrictive approach towards arbitrability. The link between court control and arbitrability is evident.

The observations made in respect of the correlation between the possibility to exercise court control and the scope of arbitrability may be extended to the matter that is relevant here, i.e. awards without reasons. Without touching the cornerstone principle that arbitral awards may not be reviewed on the merits by the controlling courts, it does not seem to be advantageous to the credibility of arbitration that awards are rendered without any explanation of the elements and reasoning that led to the decision. Quite to the contrary, the calls for transparency that have recently turned round the world of investment arbitration[24] seem to be affecting also commercial arbitration.[25] Commercial awards are being published to a larger extent than earlier,[26] institutions are being more transparent regarding the appointment and removal of arbitral tribunals,[27] and initiatives flourish to increase transparency in commercial arbitration.[28] This suggests that the general expectations towards arbitration are not going in the direction of releasing arbitral tribunals from any obligation to state the reasons for their decisions. The intention, when permitting that an award does not state reasons, is to enhance arbitration and increase its effectiveness. The risk is that exactly the opposite result is obtained, i.e. that arbitration loses its credibility and, instead of being promoted, is restricted.

IV. REASONING AND COURT CONTROL: JURISDICTION

One of the grounds for setting aside an award or refusing its enforcement is that the arbitral tribunal did not have jurisdiction. In connection with the arbitral tribunal's jurisdiction, particularly the existence and validity of the arbitration agreement, the doctrine of *Kompetenz-Kompetenz* was developed. According to this doctrine, an arbitral tribunal has the competence to decide on its own competence.[29] The main implication of this doctrine is that a tribunal does not have to suspend the proceeding in case the validity of the arbitration agreement is questioned. The arbitral tribunal has the power to make a decision on the existence and validity of the arbitration agreement and, if the decision is in the affirmative, the tribunal may proceed with the substantial aspects of the dispute.

This principle can be found in article 16 of the UNCITRAL Model Law for instance. A system that even more clearly gives priority to the arbitral tribunal's evaluation of its competence is France, where the so-called *effet négatif de la compétence-compétence* was developed.[30] According to this theory, courts must refer the dispute to arbitration whenever they are seized with a dispute which is subject to an arbitration agreement. Also under the UNCITRAL Model Law a court must refer the dispute to arbitration if there is an arbitration agreement. However, in the wording of article 8 of the Model Law, the court refers to arbitration "unless it finds that the agreement is null and void, inoperative or incapable of being performed." This wording opens for a thorough examination by the court of the existence, validity and effectiveness of the arbitration agreement. The French Civil Code of Procedure goes further and restricts the court's examination.[31] The only possibility courts have at this stage, is to make a cursory review of the arbitration agreement. If the court is *prima facie* satisfied that the arbitration agreement exists and is valid, it shall refer the dispute to arbitration. The underlying idea is that it is for the arbitral tribunal to make a deeper evaluation of its competence.

What do the Model Law and the French *effet négatif de la compétence-compétence* provide as to the issue raised in section II. above, i.e. the effects for the court of the tribunal's decision on its own competence?

The same issue of competence that was decided by the tribunal may be put forward for the purpose of challenging the validity of the award or of preventing its enforcement. The Model Law says in articles 34(2)(a)(i) that the court may set aside an award if it finds that the arbitration agreement did not exist or was invalid, or that a party was under some incapacity. The same can be said for French law: article 1492 No 1 of the Civil Procedure Code gives the court the power to set aside the award if the arbitral tribunal did not have jurisdiction. The same may be said regarding article 36(1)(a)(i) of the Model Law and article V(1)(a) of the New York Convention, in respect of enforcement. Neither the Model Law, nor the French Civil Procedure Code or the New York Convention, however, explain the relationship between the tribunal's competence to decide on its own competence, and the court's power to evaluate the validity of the arbitration agreement or the legal capacity of the parties.

According to the prevailing doctrine, the court retains its power to determine the existence and validity of the arbitration agreement, or the parties' capacity to enter into it, even if the tribunal already has evaluated the matter.[32] This may result in a different outcome from the one to which the tribunal came and may lead to setting aside the award or refusing its enforcement. In practice, this means that the award has no preclusive effect and the mentioned issues ultimately are subject to the court's evaluation. This approach is supported also in France.[33] The theories of *Kompetenz-Kompetenz* and of *l'effet négatif de la compétence-compétence,* which were developed to enhance the autonomy and thus the efficiency of arbitration, do not go as far as to affirm that the tribunal's determination of the existence and validity of the arbitration agreement are final and the court owes deference to the tribunal's determination.

The reasons stated in the award, therefore, are important to permit the court to verify on what basis the arbitral tribunal assumed jurisdiction. However, the court is not bound by the tribunal's reasoning. This does not mean that reasons are useless and may be dispensed of: by explaining the reasons for its decision on jurisdiction, the arbitral tribunal supplies the factual and legal basis upon which the decision was made, the arguments that were examined and the reasons for discarding the opposed arguments. While not bound by the tribunal's reasoning, a court will have a more complete basis for developing its own reasoning than if it had not had the benefit of the tribunal's reasons.

V. REASONING AND COURT CONTROL: PUBLIC POLICY

One of the other grounds for setting aside an award or refusing its enforcement is that the award infringes public policy. In the Model Law and in the New York Convention this ground is dealt with in the same articles as the ground relating to the arbitral tribunal's jurisdiction, that was discussed in section IV. above: challenge to the validity is regulated in article 34(2)(b)(ii) of the Model Law and refusal of enforcement in articles 36(1)(b)(ii) of the Model Law and V(2)(b) of the New York Convention.

The only difference between the provision on jurisdiction and that on public policy suggests that conflict with public policy is considered to be a more serious defect of the award than the wrong determination by the tribunal of its jurisdiction. While the ground relating to jurisdiction has to be raised by one party, the ground relating to public policy can be raised *ex officio* by the court. By giving the court the power to consider the matter of public policy *ex officio,* the applicable sources show that it is not possible to delegate to the parties the decision of whether the issue of conformity with public policy shall be considered. Moreover, it should not be possible to delegate to the tribunal the determination of whether or not public policy was infringed. The logical consequence is that the court's power to exercise its control notwithstanding the arbitral tribunal's determination of the same issue is at least equally preserved in respect of both public policy and the tribunal's jurisdiction. As was seen in section IV. above, the award does not have preclusive effects in respect of the tribunal's determination of its own competence. Similarly, there should be no preclusive effects in respect of the tribunal's determination of conformity with public policy.

However, in connection with public policy there is no unitary approach to the effects for the court of the tribunal's determination. Two opposed doctrines were developed to define the degree of control that courts may exercise on the award's conformity with public policy.[34] The Paris Court of Appeal[35] developed the minimalist doctrine, according to which courts owe deference to the tribunal's evaluation. The Dutch Court of Appeal[36] developed the maximalist doctrine, according to which courts may independently evaluate whether *ordre public* is infringed. The maximalist approach has effects that are comparable with the effects recognised by the doctrine of *compétence-compétence* and of *l'effet négatif de la compétence-compétence*; according to this approach, the court may carry out its independent evaluation of the issue. The minimalist approach goes further in affirming the finality of arbitral awards, and assumes that the tribunal's determination of the public policy issue has preclusive effects for the court.

For both approaches, the starting point is that court control is not meant to re-open the dispute that was decided by the award. In particular, the court may not review the arbitral tribunal's assessment of facts, evaluation of evidence and application of law. When the court has to determine whether the award is compatible with public policy, however, a question arises as to how far the court may go in its evaluation.

According to the maximalist approach, the court may independently evaluate whether the award leads to a result that violates public policy, irrespective of whether the arbitral tribunal already has considered the same matter. This means that the court may independently evaluate the evidence that was already evaluated by the arbitral tribunal and may form its own opinion of the disputed facts. Furthermore, the court may independently evaluate how the law shall be applied. All this is done solely for the purpose of ascertaining whether the award violates public policy. This is not made for the purpose of reviewing whether the tribunal correctly interpreted the evidence or applied the law.

The minimalist approach assumes that the court shall limit itself to verifying whether the arbitral tribunal has considered the matter. If the arbitral tribunal has concluded that public policy was not violated, the court has to accept this conclusion. Hence, according to the minimalist approach, the arbitral tribunal's evaluation of whether the award is compatible with public policy is binding on the court. The award has, therefore, preclusive effect.

The minimalist approach is particularly represented in France.[37] However, French case law recently seems to have embraced the maximalist approach, at least in areas such as corruption and money laundering.[38]

As I argue in section III. above, the maximalist approach is to be preferred, as it is more compatible with the rationale of court control. By postulating that the court owes deference to the evaluation that the tribunal made of the conformity of the award with public policy, the minimalist theory effectively delegates to the arbitral tribunal the assessment of this ground for annulment and for refusing enforcement. Thus, the minimalist approach effectively deprives court control of any possibility to exercise its functions. In my opinion, this seriously undermines the credibility of arbitration as dispute resolution mechanism, and creates a significant risk that the scope of arbitrability is restricted. As discussed in section III. above, the first signs may be seen in connection with disputes regarding EU law.

What role does this inconsistent approach play for the award's reasons?

In the minimalist approach, reasons are crucial: if the only role for the court is to determine whether the arbitral tribunal considered the matter, it is necessary that the award states reasons reflecting that the matter has been considered.

Also in the maximalist approach reasons are important. They will not prevent the court's independent consideration of the matter, but they will give an important starting point for the court's evaluation. It is generally recognised that the court's power to set aside an award or refuse its enforcement on the ground of public policy shall be exercised restrictively:[39] only fundamental principles qualify as principles of public policy, and only serious infringements of these principles justify setting aside an award or refusing its enforcement. If it is necessary to initiate a full-fledged inquiry to ascertain whether an award infringes, for example, competition law,[40] it could be argued that the infringement is not so serious as to justify applying the public policy ground.

It has been suggested[41] that it should be possible to exercise court control by examining, in some detail, the reasoning of the award. Only in exceptional cases, such as when the award has no reasons, or the award did not consider the applicability of public policy rules, should the court be allowed to go further and examine the parties' pleadings or the evidence produced in the arbitral proceedings or, in extreme cases, to launch a full-fledged investigation. This reflects the minimalist approach.

I can subscribe to this scale of court control's intensity, with one addition: in order to safeguard the efficacy of the public policy rule, I would add that the court may go further and examine the pleadings and the evidence also when the court does not find the award's reasoning convincing. With this addition, the intensity of court control corresponds to the criteria laid down by the maximalist theory. If the examination of the award or the examination of the evidence and documentation upon which the award relies gives the court reason to conclude that competition law was infringed, and that this infringement is so serious that it affects public policy, the award may be set aside or refused enforcement.

The maximalist approach is not meant to give the court the power to review the tribunal's decision. As was seen above, public policy is not violated simply because the award has wrongly applied the governing law. Even when the allegedly incorrectly applied provisions are mandatory, there is no automatic effect on public policy. Public policy is affected only if the result of the award seriously infringes fundamental values in the socio-economic system. It is, in other words, not the technical content of a legal rule that may constitute public policy, but the underlying principles. The narrow scope of the public policy rule, therefore, prevents that court control becomes a review of the merits: an award may not be set aside simply because the tribunal did not accurately apply certain rules of law.

In summary, the reasons of the award are indispensable to court control in respect of public policy if the court applies the minimalist theory. The simple circumstance that the reasons make reference to the arbitral tribunal's public policy evaluation is, under the minimalist approach, sufficient to exclude the court's authority to consider that issue. If the court applies the maximalist theory, similarly to what was said in respect of jurisdiction, the reasons are not indispensable, because the court develops its own independent evaluation of the issue. However, reasons are important because they supply the full set of arguments and evaluations upon which the award is based. Thus, the award's reasons have an important function in that they permit the court to make an informed assessment of the public policy issue, taking into due consideration the elements that were considered by the arbitral tribunal.

VI. REASONING AND COURT CONTROL: EXCESS OF POWER

Another situation in which the award's reasons are crucial, when the award is challenged or enforcement is resisted, is when the losing party alleges that the arbitral tribunal went beyond the scope of its power. The main purpose of the rule permitting annulment or refusing enforcement on the ground of excess of power is to ensure that the award is rendered within the borders set by the arbitration agreement and by the parties' pleadings. An award that goes beyond those borders is an award not based on the parties' consent to arbitrate, and is therefore invalid and unenforceable. Generally, this ground is considered to apply when the arbitral tribunal decides on matters that were not covered by the arbitration agreement or were not raised by the parties, or when it otherwise goes beyond the facts that were referred to by the parties. As an illustration may be mentioned an award ordering one party to set off its claims against claims that the other party has under a separate contract that was not subject to the arbitration agreement under which the arbitral tribunal was appointed.

This ground for annulment and for refusing enforcement applies first of all to excess in the strict sense, meaning that the tribunal decided matters beyond the borders of the dispute as was set by the parties (*ultra petita partium*). This ground, however, can apply also to the opposite situation, in which the tribunal does not consider issues presented by the parties (*infra petita partium*). While some arbitration laws, such as the UK Arbitration Act[42] and the Swiss Private International Law Act[43] expressly mention the invalidity of an award that is *infra petita*, the Model Law and the New York Convention are silent on the matter. However, case law and literature extend the ground of excess of power also to this scenario.[44]

Such an excess of power may occur in connection with the factual circumstances that the tribunal relied on, in connection with the remedies that the tribunal ordered, or in connection with the legal reasoning made by the tribunal. In all these situations, the reasons stated in the award shed light on the basis for the decision and on the relationship between the basis for the decision and the parties' pleadings. Without a reasoned award, it would be impossible for the court to understand whether the tribunal has considered the parties' pleadings and on what basis the tribunal founds its decision.

The importance of the award's reasons may be seen particularly in respect of the legal basis on which the award relies. Often, the defence of excess of power is considered to be irrelevant to the questions of law, as this is deemed to be a question relating to the merits of the dispute (and therefore immune from court control), rather than to the scope of the arbitral tribunal's power.[45] In my opinion, to the contrary, the applicable law is certainly relevant to the scope of the dispute: the scope of the dispute is mainly determined by the disputed contract, but the contract does not have legal effects simply in force of itself—it receives its legal effects from the governing law. As I have discussed elsewhere, [46] the same contract wording may have dramatically different effects depending on which law governs it. It may be argued, therefore, that the scope of the dispute is determined by the contract as construed under its applicable law. An arbitral tribunal that applies legal sources different from the law chosen by the parties in the contract may be equal to a tribunal that applies a contract wording different from the wording contained in the disputed contract. Hence, the tribunal may be deemed to have gone beyond the powers that were conferred to it under the contract.[47]

It should be pointed out, however, that in many legal systems, the arbitral tribunal is not expected to restrict its legal reasoning to the sources that were pleaded by the parties.[48] Therefore, the simple circumstance that a source was applied on the tribunal's own initiative does not constitute an excess of power. However, the right to be heard may be infringed, as will be seen in section VII. below.

Furthermore, courts do not have any power to control the tribunal's application of the law—with some notable exceptions, such as England and the United States. This becomes relevant particularly when it comes to the interpretation and application of the law in relation to the contract terms. A contract may contain terms that contradict the law that was chosen by the parties to govern it. For example, the contract may provide for payment of penalties in case of breach by a party of its obligations, and it may be governed by a law that does not consider contractual penalties to be enforceable. Whether the tribunal applies the law strictly even when this may contradict the terms of the contract, or whether it acts more flexibly and deems that contract terms must prevail even when they contradict the applicable law, is a question of the sensitivity of the particular tribunal.[49] The courts have no say, as long as this remains a question of merits, i.e. a question of the tribunal's interpretation and construction of the contract and of its application of the law. The courts would have jurisdiction, however, if the arbitration agreement or the parties' common instructions contained restrictions as to the tribunal's power to apply the law. However, the parties usually do not attempt to restrict the tribunal's power with regard to the impact that the governing law may have on the interpretation and construction of the contract.[50]

However, the review of the tribunal's application of the law, which courts are not allowed to make, should be distinguished from the review of whether the tribunal had the power to apply a certain law. The courts have the power to make this latter review.

In particular, this is important in situations where the dispute arises out of a contract that contains a clause choosing a certain governing law, but the arbitral award takes into consideration provisions from other laws as well. The typical example would be a contract between parties belonging to two EU States and having effects on the EU market, but containing a clause choosing as governing law the law of a non-EU State. If the contract violates the EU competition law, for example, the arbitral tribunal may be forced to consider EU competition law in order to avoid rendering an award that infringes public policy (see section V. above). Usually, competition law would be invoked as a defence by the party who did not comply with the contract. The argument would be that breach of the contractual obligation may not be sanctioned, because the obligation was invalid as it infringed EU-competition law. However, the arbitral tribunal may also raise the question of infringement of EU-competition law *ex officio*. If the arbitral tribunal applies a law different from the law chosen by the parties, however, it may be deemed to have exceeded its power. It is, therefore, necessary to verify whether the tribunal has the power to apply a law different from the law that was chosen by the parties, or whether this goes beyond the powers that the parties conferred on the tribunal.

Whether the arbitral tribunal exceeds its power or not, depends on the reasoning that led to disregarding the choice of law made in the contract. If the tribunal does not justify its application of a non-chosen law, there is a basis for considering the award to be in excess of the power that the parties conferred on the tribunal. However, where the legal reasoning gives a basis for applying a law different from the law chosen by the parties, there is no excess of power.[51]

As I have discussed elsewhere, there are at least two approaches: the traditional one, that is often frowned upon as being old fashioned and unfriendly to arbitration, but that in my opinion is the most arbitration-friendly approach;[52] and the modern one, that is often deemed to be the most progressive and arbitration-friendly, but that in my opinion creates unpredictable results and endangers the creditworthiness of arbitration as a dispute resolution method.[53] The traditional approach uses the private international law to explain the arbitral tribunal's power to consider laws different from the law chosen by the parties. The modern approach considers that the tribunal has full discretion to consider any law, without the necessity to justify the selection of the law (the so-called *voie directe*).

According to the traditional approach, the parties' or the arbitral tribunal's choice of law is the exercise of a power regulated by that branch of the law that goes under the name of private international law (also known as conflict of laws, or choice of law rules).

In the field of international arbitration, some specific private international law rules are codified in international conventions,[54] whereas others are regulated in national arbitration law. Of particular interest in the transnational context may be the 2015 Principles of Choice of Law in International Contracts,[55] published by the Hague Conference and meant as a restatement of generally recognised principles of private international law.

Regarding the law applicable to the merits of the dispute, which is the relevant issue here, national arbitration law is harmonised by the UNCITRAL Model Law and contains a choice of law rule giving the parties the possibility to choose the applicable law.[56] In case the parties have not made use of their party autonomy, the UNCITRAL Model law directs the arbitral tribunal to apply the conflict rules that the tribunal "considers applicable".[57] The Model Law, thus, follows the traditional approach and applies the private international law mechanism. However, in the revision of 2006, the Model Law received a more flexible version and was emancipated from the automatic application of the private international law of the state where the tribunal has its venue. This was meant to cater for situations where the venue of arbitration has no connection with the dispute, and where it may be appropriate to apply the conflict rules of states with closer connection. In practice, in many situations, arbitral tribunals may still consider the venue of the arbitration as a significant connecting factor and thus apply its conflict rules to determine the law applicable to the merits of the dispute.[58]

However, not all jurisdictions have adopted the Model Law's reference to private international law (of the venue or otherwise): some jurisdictions provide a specific conflict rule for arbitration,[59] some contain no guidelines at all,[60] and some regulate the so-called *voie directe*,[61] that does not rely on private international law and gives no criteria for the selection of the applicable law. It cannot be excluded that arbitral tribunals will make use of private international law even when the arbitration is subject to an arbitration law that does not regulate the selection of law or provides for the *voie directe:* although not required to apply conflict rules, arbitral tribunals may find that the well-known mechanism of private international law permits to select the law more objectively and predictably than mere discretion without guidelines. Even though conflict rules may be complicated and sometimes they may leave room for discretion, the abundant literature and case law on the area contribute to rendering its application quite predictable.

With the exception of the latter mentioned approach, the *voie directe*, (that is the starting point for the modern approach discussed below), this short overview shows that the private international law has still a quite important role in arbitration.[62] Even those who deem it undesirable to apply a national system of private international law, can find acceptable the mechanism underlying private international law in generally acknowledged principles such as the Hague Principles on Choice of Law.[63]

It is therefore justified to look at the private international law as the framework for determining the scope of the choice of law made by the parties and selected by the arbitral tribunal. As the choice of law is the exercise of a power based on private international law, any restrictions or exceptions that rely on principles or rules of private international law do not violate the parties' choice of law; they simply implement the parties' choice of law pursuant to its scope as determined in the legal sources upon which it is based.

One of the restrictions that are relevant to the arbitral tribunal's power to consider a law different from the law chosen by the parties, is that the parties' choice in private international law generally applies only within the scope of contract law (and to a certain extent also tort law). If a dispute has implications of company law or property law, or if it is on areas where states exercise their regulatory powers such as competition law (also known as overriding mandatory rules or *lois de police*), the court will apply the law chosen by the parties to the contractual issues of the dispute, and to the other aspects it will apply the law selected according to the appropriate conflict rules (so-called *dépeçage*).

It has been suggested that party autonomy in arbitration has a wider scope than party autonomy in private international law.[64] In arbitration law, often the parties are permitted to choose the law applicable not only to the contract, but more generally to the *merits* of the dispute—as an example, the UNCITRAL Model Law says that the parties may choose the law applicable to the substance of the dispute. This is interpreted as giving party autonomy a wider scope than the one party autonomy has in private international law as described above: if the dispute has implications that go beyond the mere contract law, according to this opinion party autonomy would also cover these aspects. According to this logic, therefore, the private international law would not be a sufficient basis to justify the arbitral tribunal's power to override the parties' choice of law: the parties' choice of law would not be restricted to the mere contract matters, but would extend to any issues within the scope of the dispute.

However, although the wording of arbitration law may seem wider than, for example, the wording of the Rome I Regulation—according to which the parties may choose the law applicable not to the *merits* of the dispute, but only to *contractual obligations*—it may be questioned whether this can be taken as a basis for assuming that the parties in arbitration have the power to choose the law applicable to matters of company law, property law or regulatory matters. This is because the choice of law possible in arbitration relates to the merits of the *dispute.* Therefore, it must be interpreted within the scope of the dispute that may be decided by the arbitral tribunal. Generally, arbitration may decide disputes between the parties on rights and obligations that the parties may dispose of, and decides the dispute with effects for the parties. An arbitral tribunal may not render an award with effects for third parties: therefore, an arbitral award will not be empowered to decide that the resolution of a company body is invalid, or that a certain asset of the insolvent debtor is not available to the generality of the creditors. These aspects, being outside of the dispute, cannot be covered by the broad language of the conflict rule for arbitration. A dispute may have implications of, for example, company law, property law or competition law, but these issues will not be the direct object of the claim. They will be preliminary issues that the tribunal may consider in the course of its determination of the claim. For example, a claim for reimbursement of damages due to breach of contract may require that the tribunal examines whether the board resolution upon which the contract was signed was valid, or whether the contract was valid under competition law. The dispute, however, will not become a dispute of company law or of competition law: it will be a dispute of contract law, for the decision of which the tribunal must consider some preliminary issues. The scope of the dispute, and therefore its merits, are defined by the claim, and the claim is, in our example, a contractual claim. The wording of the choice of law rule contained in the Model Law, therefore, does not seem to extend the scope of party autonomy in a significant manner.

If the choice made by the parties is not unlimited, it becomes necessary to find a source regulating the scope of party autonomy. Article 28 (2) of the Model Law refers to private international law for the eventuality that the parties have not chosen the law. However, it is systematically correct to use the same reference also for the purpose of specifying the scope of party autonomy in article 28 (1). Where else should the source regulating the details of party autonomy be found? The Model Law itself does not give crucial elements such as the parameters for a valid exercise of party autonomy, the specification of its scope, or its effects. All these elements are to be found in the private international law, and it is only natural to refer to the private international law that is referred to in article 28 (2) also for the purpose of article 28 (1).

In summary, a systematic interpretation of the sources applicable to arbitration, including also the private international law, seems to give justification for the arbitral tribunal's power to consider rules of competition law not belonging to the law that was chosen by the parties.[65]

The relevance of private international law mechanisms in arbitration, however, is not uncontroversial. Private international law has been, in my opinion, unjustly considered an excessively rigid and old-fashioned mechanism detrimental to the effectiveness of arbitration. On this basis, it has been discarded in various jurisdictions in favour of more flexible approaches meant to enhance the prominence of party autonomy—such as the *voie directe,* contained, inter alia, in article 1511 of the French Code of Civil Procedure, in article 27a of the Swedish Arbitration Act, as well as in numerous Arbitration Rules;—including also the UNCITRAL Rules. Indeed, giving the arbitral tribunal full discretion to apply whatever sources the tribunal deems appropriate, provides the tribunal with unlimited flexibility. This, however, is not necessarily positive.

A first reason why a flexible approach is not necessarily desirable is that it may lead to unpredictable results. If the arbitral tribunal is not guided by objective criteria when it determines the applicable law, the parties are not in a position to assess in advance their respective legal positions and thus evaluate the advisability of initiating the arbitration. In some cases, determining the applicable law in advance is essential to the evaluation of whether to start an arbitral proceeding or not. For example, whether the applicable law will be Italian or Norwegian will decide whether a four years old claim is time barred or not, as the period of limitations is 10 years under Italian law and 3 years under Norwegian law. If the criteria for determining the applicable law are not objective, the parties are put in the paradoxical situation of having to initiate an arbitration to be able to assess whether there is at all a basis for initiating arbitration.

A second reason why a flexible approach to determining the applicable law is not necessarily desirable is that, without conflict of laws rules, the tribunal has no legal basis upon which it may restrict the choice of law made by the parties. This becomes relevant when the choice of law made by the parties leads to disregarding overriding mandatory rules or principles of public policy in the law(s) that would be applicable if the parties had not made a choice of law. While the traditional approach founds the arbitral tribunal's selection of the applicable law on the private international law, the *voie directe* does not provide a legal basis. This may seem to suggest that party autonomy is not restricted by the private international law. Hence, this seems to suggest that party autonomy is unlimited. Therefore, not having a basis to restrict the parties' choice, the tribunal may fear that the award will be invalid or unenforceable for excess of power if it does not follow the parties' choice, for example by considering competition law. To justify the arbitral tribunal's power to consider laws different from the law chosen by the parties, it has been suggested that the arbitral tribunal has an ethical duty to consider applicable overriding mandatory rules, also taking into account the necessity to preserve the credibility of arbitration.[66] The specific content of this ethical duty is not readily determinable, therefore it has been suggested that arbitral tribunals should exercise their discretion with a certain pragmatism and shall look at the criteria that would be applied by courts. As a result, it seems that this approach does not differ significantly from the traditional approach based on private international law.[67]

However, if the tribunal has no legal framework to contain the parties' choice, the result may be that arbitration lends itself to practices that violate fundamental principles in the international community. This is not desirable, at least for two reasons. First, it may lead to rendering an award that is invalid or unenforceable because it violates the court's public policy. Second, as I argue in section III. above, it undermines the credibility of arbitration as a method for settling disputes—because it makes arbitration a means to evade applicable mandatory regulation of fundamental character.

The reasons of the award, in summary, are crucial to the court's evaluation of the tribunal's authority to apply a law that was not chosen by the parties. If the arbitral tribunal bluntly disregards the parties' choice, it exceeds its power. If it exercises its power to select the applicable law, it does not exceed its authority.

It may not always be easy to determine the borderline between the review of the tribunal's application of the law and the decision as to whether the tribunal had the authority to apply that law. The former is not within the scope of the jurisdiction of the court. The latter may be evaluated by the courts when determining whether the arbitral tribunal exceeded the power that it was granted by the parties. This judicial control has to be based on a careful analysis of the reasons for the award to verify that the proper criteria for the exercise of the defence are met.

VII. REASONING AND COURT CONTROL: RIGHT TO BE HEARD

Another ground for invalidity and unenforceability of awards is violation of a party's right to be heard. For what interests us here, the allegation that the right to be heard was violated overlaps often with the ground of excess of power that was discussed in section VI. above. In particular, it might overlap with the allegation that one party was taken by surprise by the basis for the tribunal's decision, and was thus deprived of the possibility to present its case from the point of view that was assumed by the arbitral tribunal.

Also the ground relating to the right to be heard can be applied to a situation in which the tribunal based its decision on a legal reasoning that was not pleaded or did not consider one or more issues pleaded by a party (an award *infra petita partium*), as it is generally assumed that the right to be heard implies a duty by the tribunal to listen.[68]

A party may have been taken by surprise if the tribunal relied on facts or sources that were not pleaded by the parties, or if the tribunal applied the sources in a manner that did not correspond to the parties' pleadings. Not having expected that the tribunal would base its decision on those elements or on that reasoning, the parties did not make their comments thereon and were deprived of the possibility to present new arguments or evidence that they might have presented if they had known that a certain fact would be considered or that a certain source would be applied by the tribunal.

It must be pointed out that, in some systems, arbitral tribunals have the power to develop their own legal arguments and are not expected to request the parties to comment on the tribunal's legal reasoning.[69] However, even in those systems, the tribunal's room for independent legal reasoning may be restricted if the parties may be deemed to have been taken by surprise by the application of a certain source.[70]

The award's reasons can contribute to verifying whether the parties were given the possibility to present their respective cases, whether they had the possibility to expect the application of the sources upon which the decision relied, and whether the parties' pleadings were taken into due consideration.

VIII. REASONING AND COURT CONTROL: DUE PROCESS

Regarding the grounds for setting aside an award or refusing its enforcement on the basis that procedural errors were made, the award's reasons are not as crucial as they are in respect of the grounds discussed in the previous sections. However, reasons may be very helpful, because they may constitute a record of the procedural history that can be used to evaluate whether errors were committed during the proceedings.

It is possible that a party challenges the validity of an award or resists its enforcement—for example, alleging that it was discriminated against because it was given less time than the other party to present its evidence; or alleging that an arbitrator was not independent; or objecting to the decision on costs in the award.[71] These allegations may, depending on the circumstances, be groundless. For example, one party may have been given less time than the other to present its evidence because that party's evidence was produced in the language of the proceedings, while the other party's evidence needed to be translated. In such a situation, the different time frame granted to the parties does not reflect a discrimination but reinstates equality of treatment between the parties. The challenge to the independence of the arbitrator may have been made too late, for example because the challenging party was asked, in the course of the proceedings, to comment on a certain circumstance regarding the independence of the arbitrator, and failed to object at that time. If the party waited to challenge the arbitrator until after the award had been rendered, it may have lost the right to invoke that circumstance. The fees of the arbitrators may be very high compared to the value of the dispute, but this may be due to excessive work that the arbitral tribunal was forced to do because of numerous and groundless requests made by the party who challenged the fees.

In all these situations, and many others, it is possible to provide evidence that the invoked circumstances are not grounds for invalidity and unenforceability. However, this requires a considerable work for the other party and the court, who are expected to collect evidence that may be scattered among hundreds of e-mails exchanged during the proceedings, and to deduce from them what were the reasons for the arbitral tribunal's conduct. If the award contains reasons, and the reasons have a section explaining the procedural history, it becomes much simpler for the controlling court to follow how the proceedings were conducted and to take a decision on whether the circumstances justified the tribunal's conduct or whether the award shall be set aside or refused enforcement.

IX. ARE THE REASONS OF AN AWARD DISPENSABLE?

It was seen in section I. above that arbitration is under pressure to become a more efficient process. Recent developments such as the creation of the role of the emergency arbitrator testify to the desire to ensure that arbitration is capable of speedy responses to the needs of the parties. Many arbitration institutions have added rules for expedited proceedings to their rules for ordinary proceedings.[72] Expedited proceedings are meant to be completed in a shorter time frame than ordinary proceedings. A number of measures permits a more expedited conduct of the proceedings: for example, the number of exchanges of submissions that are to take place between the parties may be reduced, the tribunal may be given the discretion to decide the case on the basis of written submissions only, the deadlines for writing the award may be reduced, etc.

The measures to enhance efficiency may also affect the reasons of the award. For example, under the Stockholm Rules for Expedited Arbitration, the award is to state reasons only if one of the parties so requests.[73] This means that, under these rules, the base case is that an award needs not state reasons.

Most rules for expedited arbitration have not gone so far, and awards are usually expected to state reasons even in expedited proceedings. The ICC Expedited Procedure Rules,[74] for example, do not permit to derogate from article 32 (2) of the Arbitration Rules, according to which awards must state the reasons upon which they are based.[75] As a matter of fact, the ICC Notes to the Parties and Arbitral Tribunals state that: "Any award under the Expedited Procedure Provisions shall be reasoned. Arbitral tribunals may limit the factual and/or procedural sections of the award to what they consider to be necessary to the understanding of the award, and state the reasons of the award in as concise a fashion as possible." In my experience as member of the ICC Court of Arbitration, the scrutiny of the draft awards rendered under the Expedited Procedures takes into consideration the need for an expedited processing, but is no less thorough in substance than for ordinary arbitration.

The UNCITRAL Working Group II on dispute resolution, which is currently working on matters relating to expedited arbitration, discussed at its 69th session in February 2019 whether it is desirable to eliminate the requirement that the award states the reasons for the decision.[76] The outcome of the discussion was not favourable to eliminating the requirement, but the simple fact that the matter was discussed, shows that measures are contemplated for the purpose of enhancing efficiency.

In a similar vein, for ordinary (non-expedited) arbitration proceedings the UNCITRAL Model Law on International Commercial Arbitration permits the parties to agree that the award shall not state any reasons.[77] This is a less drastic solution than the described approach in the Stockholm Rules for Expedited Arbitration. While the Stockholm rules require that one party actively requests that the award states reasons, the Model Law requires that both parties actively agree to exclude the reasons. This should be seen as a hommage to the primacy of party autonomy, rather than as a measure to enhance efficiency. In the quest for efficiency that inspires contemporary arbitration, however, the possibility for the parties to agree on discarding the reasons may become an appealing option.

As was discussed in the previous sections, however, the reasons of the award may be necessary for the purpose of rendering court control meaningful. Given that the award's reasons are necessary or important to permit court control, how can this be reconciled with the systems that permit the parties to agree that the award shall not state any reasons, or even that assume that awards shall not have reasons unless one party requests so? As an award that does not state reasons prevents or at least hampers court control, it must be assumed that an award without reasons will not be deemed acceptable by a court. Permitting the parties to exclude reasons may create considerable problems if the applicable arbitration law does not permit to exclude court control, and may create difficulties in case of enforcement.

In some systems, such as under Swedish law, awards do not need to state reasons,[78] and the parties furthermore are allowed to waive the right to challenge the validity of the award.[79] Therefore, the Stockholm rules are not inconsistent with the applicable arbitration law, when they assume that awards shall not have reasons unless one party requires so. However, under the Model Law, the parties may not waive their right to challenge the validity of the award. How can this be reconciled with the possibility that the Model Law gives to the parties to agree on having an award without reasons? When the reasons are necessary to evaluate the validity of the award, how to interpret the parties' agreement that the award shall not state reasons? Is it an indirect way of waiving the right to challenge which, however, may not be waived under the applicable arbitration law? Or is it a reason to consider the award invalid, because it prevents the court from exercising control? The inconsistency in the system is evident. [80]

The same inconsistency applies to enforcement of the award: the New York Convention does not permit the parties to waive their right to resist enforcement.[81] The losing party may, of course, elect not to resist enforcement, thus achieving the same result as if it had waived the right to resist. However, an agreement in which a party commits itself in advance not to resist enforcement in case it loses, is not contemplated in the New York Convention. If an award is without reasons, therefore, there is a possibility that its enforceability is at risk.

The foregoing seems to suggest that it is not advisable for the parties to agree on an award without reasons. While it may be tempting to expedite the award by doing away with its reasons, the final result may be far less efficient than if the tribunal had been given some additional weeks to draft reasons—as the award may run the risk of being set aside or refused enforcement. If the award may not be carried out, it does not help much that it was rendered within a short timeframe.

X. WHAT STANDARD SHOULD BE MET WHEN STATING THE REASONS OF THE AWARD?

The foregoing shows what is necessary or advisable to address in the award, for the sake of preserving its validity and enforceability. However, there does not seem to be a general standard applicable to international arbitration,[82] and in any case the level of detail will depend on the characteristics of the dispute. A simple dispute based mainly on the evaluation of evidence will not require as extensive legal analysis as a dispute presenting various legal issues; a dispute in which the parties have a high level of litigiousness will require a more detailed procedural history than a dispute in which both parties acted seriously and professionally, etc.

It is advisable to write reasons that not only meet the requirement of court control, but also explain to the parties, in a convincing manner, the basis for the decision. This, however, does not mean that the award shall be written with the aim of developing the law and becoming a precedent for future disputes. Considering that in commercial arbitration the priority is still efficiency, it does not seem advisable to significantly exceed the standard that is necessary to satisfy court control. The style of investment awards, therefore, is not necessarily to be followed for commercial awards. The arbitral tribunal should strive to strike a reasonable balance between the two extremes: an award that does nothing more than ordering one party to pay a certain amount, on one hand, and an award that constitutes a treatise on the matters at issue, on the other hand.

A reasonable balance suggests that an award contains:

(i) **Reference to the arbitration agreement, as well as an explanation of the basis upon which the tribunal assumed jurisdiction on the dispute.** If the jurisdiction was contested, the award should refer to the applicable sources of law that constitute a basis for jurisdiction. As was seen in section IV. above, the controlling courts have an independent power to determine whether the tribunal have jurisdiction. However, the reasoning of the award will be the starting point for the court's considerations. For example, the existence of the arbitration agreement will depend on the formal requirements in the arbitration law at the place of arbitration, as well as on the evidence examined by the arbitral tribunal. If the award gives the relevant details, the annulment or the enforcement court will have a full basis to evaluate the matter. Furthermore, a party may be deemed to have lost its right to invoke that the arbitral tribunal did not have jurisdiction, if that party had the possibility to object to jurisdiction during the proceedings, but elected not to do so within the given term. A detailed reference in the award to the communication that has been made on this matter during the proceedings, constitutes an important basis for the court's evaluation of the parties' conduct and its decision on whether a party lost its right to challenge jurisdiction or not;

(ii) **A description of all steps that led to the appointment of the arbitral tribunal.** Similarly as to what was mentioned in respect of the loss of the right to invoke that the arbitral tribunal lacked jurisdiction, also in respect of the right to challenge the constitution of the arbitral tribunal, a party may lose its right if it does not present its objections before the term set for doing so during the proceedings. If the award refers to any communication that was made during the proceedings on, for example, the qualifications or the independence of the arbitrators, the court will be able to verify whether later challenges are timely or not;

(iii) **A description of the procedural history.** As was seen in section VIII. above, a thorough description of the proceedings may contribute to the effectiveness of the award as it provides the court with a basis to verify the regularity of the procedure. It happens, sometimes, that a party is particularly litigious, possibly giving rise to the suspicion that it is trying to delay the proceedings—for example, it presents numerous unfounded requests to extend the terms, it objects to all procedural decisions taken by the tribunal, it requests discovery of voluminous evidence that is not relevant, etc. The award should record all the parties' requests and objections, and it should explain the reasons for its decision on each of them. The award should refrain from characterising or commenting on the parties' conduct beyond giving objective explanations of the reasons for admitting or rejecting the requests and objections. Tempting as it may be under some circumstances, any non-objective comment may expose the award to being challenged on the basis that the arbitral tribunal did not act in an impartial way. This does not mean that the tribunal shall succumb to the so-called due process paranoia and accept, out of fear for infringing that party's right to due process, any abusive conduct by the parties. It means that any decision taken by the arbitral tribunal to prevent dilatory tactics should be motivated with objective reasons;

(iv) **A description of the facts upon which the decision is made.** This description has the double purpose of making it possible to follow the reasoning upon which the decision is based, and to show that the arbitral tribunal has taken into due consideration the facts invoked by each of the parties. To be useful, therefore, the description should be functional and provide a basis for the legal issues that are decided in the award. Facts that are not relevant to the legal issues, or details that are not necessary for illuminating the legal issues, should not be referred to. If the parties have made reference to irrelevant facts or to an excessively high degree of details, the award may make reference to that when it comments on the parties' respective positions (item (v) below), explaining why those facts are deemed irrelevant or the level of detail excessive;

(v) **A description of the parties' position and the remedies requested by each of the parties.** Also this description has the double purpose of making it possible to follow the reasoning upon which the decision is based, and to show that the arbitral tribunal has taken into due consideration the arguments presented by each of the parties. Often, this part of the award incorporates *verbatim* the parties' written statements. This is made in part to save time, because copying and pasting the parties' pleadings is quicker than reformulating the parties' arguments. In part, however, this is made also to avoid being criticised for having overlooked some of the parties' arguments. In my opinion, copying and pasting the parties' arguments is not an effective measure against the possible criticism that certain arguments were not considered. This only achieves to push the criticism forward: while the part of the award that incorporates the parties' pleadings is exhaustive, the part of the award containing the reasoning will reveal if one argument has not been considered. In my opinion, it is better to summarise the parties' arguments in the award, rather than copying them. Certainly, the arbitral tribunal will thoroughly study the parties' arguments, possibly taking notes for its own understanding and to structure the case. In my experience, these notes are quite easy to be transformed into a summary of the parties' main pleadings. A summary like this would render the award more readable than the copy-paste exercise, and does not require much more work than what the arbitrator anyway has to do for the purpose of understanding the case. If a tribunal is concerned with ensuring that the description captures the main arguments presented by each of the parties, it may circulate this description and ask the parties to comment thereon;

(vi) **A description of the tribunal's reasoning.** This part should address the parties' main factual and legal arguments, making specific reference to the invoked evidence and the arguments of each of the parties, and explaining the tribunal's opinion on each of these arguments. The award should refrain from making non-objective or even sarcastic comments on the arguments of the parties, and even arguments that are not convincing at all should be given due consideration. If an argument is manifestly irrelevant, illogical or unfounded, it will not be necessary to spend many sentences to dismiss it; but the dismissal should be objective and respectful. This part of the award should also explain the tribunal's legal reasoning, identifying the legal sources that it applies, explaining how it selected them and how they are applied to the facts. The award should be precise in making reference to the applicable law. Arbitral tribunals are often under the impression of being empowered to apply the law more flexibly than national courts of law. It is correct that an award remains valid and enforceable even if it has applied the law wrongly. However, as seen in sections VI. and VII. above, an award runs the risk of being in excess of power or infringing a party's right to be heard if it applied a law different from the law chosen by the parties without explaining the legal basis for this application;

(vii) **The determination of the arbitration costs,** containing also an evaluation of the reasonableness of the parties' costs if they are to be allocated between them, the indication of the criteria for determining the fees of the arbitral tribunal and of the institution, if any, as well as an explanation of how the costs have been allocated between the parties;

(viii) **The dispositive.** The dispositive should be clear and self-sufficient: it should be possible to enforce the award on the simple basis of the dispositive. The only purpose of the dispositive should be to constitute the basis for enforcement. Therefore, the dispositive should have no evaluations, arguments or explanations, but only orders or determinations (including also the determination that the tribunal has or does not have jurisdiction). Furthermore, all parameters for determining the amount of payments or for enforcing other ordered remedies should be identified or identifiable in the dispositive. The enforcing court should not be expected to interpret the contract or to evaluate the quality of a delivery or other performance. All evaluations should be made in the body of the award, and the dispositive should make the specific orders and determinations that follow from the considerations made in the body of the award. The only open issues in the dispositive should be capable of being determined in a mechanical way—for example, the amount due as interest should be determined or determinable on the basis of the criteria contained in the dispositive: a specific date for when the calculation starts, the final date for the calculation (usually, the date of actual payment), and the rate quoted in a specific source on that date. It is also useful to specify, in the dispositive, that all claims that are not reflected in the dispositive are to be deemed rejected. This prevents that new arbitral proceedings be initiated on the basis of the same claims that were the basis for the dispute decided in the award.

XI. CONCLUSION

The foregoing shows that the award's reasons are necessary to permit the court to exercise control over the compatibility of the award with public policy (if one adheres to the minimalist doctrine), as well as over the arbitral tribunal's exercise of its power (particularly in case the tribunal considered sources different from the law chosen by the parties or the sources pleaded by the parties).

If the court adheres to the maximalist theory, the award's reasons permit the court to develop its own evaluation of the public policy issue considering all elements that were considered by the arbitral tribunal. This applies also to the court's determination of the arbitral tribunal's jurisdiction.

Furthermore, the award's reasons are important to permit the court to exercise control over the proceedings' compatibility with the right to be heard and other principles of due process. The reasons of the award, therefore, should not be sacrificed in the name of more efficient arbitration proceedings.

Efficiency of the proceedings, however, is an important concern in commercial arbitration. Therefore, it does not seem appropriate to adopt the same style of drafting reasons that is customary for investment awards. Having to strike the balance between the desire to write extensive reasons capable of contributing to the development of the law and the need to ensure efficient proceedings, the reasons for commercial awards should be sufficient to permit court control, but need not exceed the requirements set by the necessity to permit court control.

NOTES

1. For an updated status, see UNCITRAL, Status, Convention on the Recognition and Enforcement of Foreign Arbitral Awards, http://www.uncitral.org/uncitral/en/uncitral_texts/arbitration/NY-Convention_status.html .
2. Convention on the Recognition and Enforcement of Foreign Arbitral Awards (adopted 10 June 1958, entered into force 7 June 1959) UNTS (New York Convention).
3. UNCITRAL, Model Law on International Commercial Arbitration, http://www.uncitral.org/pdf/english/texts/arbitration/ml-arb/07-86998_Ebook.pdf .
4. For an updated status, see UNCITRAL, Status, Model Law on International Commercial Arbitration, http://www.uncitral.org/uncitral/en/uncitral_texts/arbitration/1985Model_arbitration_status.html .
5. Gary Born, "International Commercial Arbitration", 2nd ed., *Kluwer Law International* 2014, pp. 3186, 3340; Giuditta Cordero-Moss, *International Commercial Contracts*, Cambridge University Press 2014, p. 224.
6. The European Court of Human Rights has repeatedly affirmed that, while an unmotivated verdict in criminal cases in itself is not a violation of the principle of fair trial, the principle of fair trial is breached by a process that does not provide sufficient guarantees to rule out any risk of arbitrariness and enable the accused to understand the reasons for his conviction. *Taxquet v Belgium*, Grand Chamber judgment of 16.11.2010, as well as *Agnelet v France* and *Legillon v France*, both of 10.1.2013.
7. Born, "International Commercial Arbitration", cit., p. 3042.
8. Giuditta Cordero-Moss, "EU Overriding Mandatory Provisions and the Law Applicable to the Merits", in Franco Ferrari (ed.), *The impact of EU law on international commercial arbitration*, Juris 2017, pp. 317-349, 328ff; Giuditta Cordero-Moss, "Inherent Powers and Competition Law", in F. Ferrari (ed.*), Inherent Powers in International Adjudication*, Juris 2018, pp. 297-325; Giuditta Cordero-Moss, "Mitsubishi: Balancing Arbitrability and Court Control", in Horatia Muir Watt, Lucia Bíziková, Agatha Brandão de Oliveira and Diego Fernández Arroyo (eds.), *Global Private International Law, Adjudication without Frontiers*, Elgar 2019, pp. 82-91.
9. Case C-352/13 *CDC Hydrogen Peroxide v Evonik Degussa and Others*, opinion of AG Jääskinen.
10. Case C-567/14 *Genentech v Hoechst and Sanofi-Aventis Deutschland*, opinion of AG Wathelet .
11. Case C-284/16 *Slovak Republic v Achmea BV*.
12. Bundesgerichtshof, 3.3.2016, I ZB 2/1.
13. *Achmea B.V. (former Eureko B.V.) v The Slovak Republic*, UNCITRAL, PCA Case No. 2008-13, 7.12.2012.
14. *Mitsubishi Motors Corp. v Soler Chrysler-Plymouth, Inc.*, 473 U.S. 614, 628 (1985).
15. Case C-281/16 (*Achmea*) Opinion of AG Wathelet, paras 70–72; ibid paras 251–60. The principal argument in the Opinion is that investment arbitral tribunals meet the criteria contained in article 267 TFEU. Therefore, they are permitted to request the CJEU to give a preliminary ruling and are required to apply EU law, see paras 84–135. Supporting this position, Jürgen Basedow, "EU Law in International Arbitration: Referrals to the European Court of Justice" (2015) 32(4) *Journal of International Arbitration* 367. The CJEU, however, has rejected this argument, see footnote below.
16. C-281/16 (Achmea).
17. Following the CJEU decision the BGH set aside the Achmea award on 31 October 2018.
18. Giuditta Cordero-Moss, "Achmea's distinction between investment and commercial arbitration", *The future of arbitration in Europe",* forthcoming.
19. OGH 1.3.2017, 5ob 72/16y, Ecolex 520 (2017).
20. Cour de Cassation, 16.11.2006, PAS. 2006, I, No. 11; Cour de Cassation, 14.1.2010, PAS. 2010, I, No. 12; Cour de Cassation, 3.11.2011 PAS. 2011, I, No. 1.
21. Bundesgerichtshof, 5.9.2012, Neue juristische Wochenschrift (2012).
22. *Accentuate Limited v Asigra Inc*. [2009] EWHC (QB) 2655.
23. Or they deny the recognition of a contractual choice of forum in favour of a court not located within the EU. This responds to the same rationale, i.e. that matters relating to commercial agency shall be decided by courts located in the EU in order to ensure a uniform application of EU law. Therefore, it can be expected that the same courts would also deny arbitrability if the contract contained an arbitration clause.
24. In the field of investment arbitration a significant development was made in 2013, when the UNCITRAL adopted the UNCITRAL Rules on Transparency in Treaty-based Investor-State Arbi-

tration, http://www.uncitral.org/pdf/english/texts/arbitration/arb-rules-2013/UNCITRAL-Arbitration-Rules-2013-e.pdf. A new provision was added in article 1, paragraph 4 of the UNCITRAL Arbitration Rules (that had been revised in 2010), to incorporate the Rules on Transparency for arbitration initiated pursuant to an investment treaty concluded on or after 1 April 2014. The 2014 Mauritius Convention on Transparency (https://uncitral.un.org/en/texts/arbitration/conventions/transparency) is an instrument by which Parties to investment treaties concluded before 1 April 2014 express their consent to apply the Rules on Transparency also to disputes based on investment treaties concluded prior to 1 April 2014.

25. In 2016 the then Lord Chief Justice of England and Wales, Lord Thomas, held a lecture in which he pointed out that, since many commercial parties choose arbitration to solve their disputes and appeal from arbitral awards is very restricted, courts are not participating to the desirable extent to the development of the law: Lord Thomas of Cwmgiedd, Lord Chief Justice of England and Wales, "Bailii Lecture: Developing Commercial Law through the Courts: Rebalancing the Relationship between the Courts and Arbitration" (March 9, 2016). The same criticism had been put forward, decades earlier, by the then Chief Justice of the Norwegian Supreme Court, Carsten Smith. "Voldgift—domstolenes konkurrent og hjelper", in *Tidsskrift for Rettsvitenskap,* 1993, p. 474ff. The Norwegian Arbitration Act of 2004 acted upon this criticism and assumes that confidentiality of the awards must be agreed to by the parties. In contrast, most arbitration laws still assume confidentiality as the main rule in arbitration.

26. Many arbitration institutions publish, in anonymised version, a selection of the awards rendered under their rules. For example, following an amendment to the ICC Notes to the parties and arbitral tribunals on the conduct of the arbitration under the ICC Arbitration Rules dated 1 January 2019, https://cdn.iccwbo.org/content/uploads/sites/3/2017/03/icc-note-to-parties-and-arbitral-tribunals-on-the-conduct-of-arbitration.pdf, all awards rendered after 1 January 2019 may be published, unless one party objects. In addition, awards are collected in data bases such as the database Case Law on UNCITRAL Texts (CLOUT, https://www.uncitral.org/clout/) or the database on UNIDROIT Principles and CISG Unilex (http://www.unilex.info/).

27. See, for example, the publication by the Stockholm Arbitration Institute in 2017 of its policy for appointing arbitrators: https://sccinstitute.com/media/220131/scc-policy-appointment-of-arbitrators-2017.pdf .

28. See, for example, *Arbitrator Intelligence*, https://www.arbitratorintelligence.org/ .

29. Born, "International Commercial Arbitration", cit., paras 1046-1252; Christophe Seraglini and Jérôme Ortscheidt, "Droit de l'arbitrage interne et international", Domat Montchrestien, 2013, paras 664f. See also John James Barcelo, "Kompetenz-Kompetenz and Its Negative Effect—A Comparative View", *Cornell Legal Studies Research Paper* No. 17-40, 11 September 2017, Available at SSRN: https://ssrn.com/abstract=3035485.

30. Emmanuel Gaillard and John Savage (eds.), "Fouchard Gaillard Goldman on International Commercial Arbitration", *Kluwer Law* 1999, paras 660, 671 ff.; Emmanuel Gaillard, "L'effet négatif de la compétence-compétence", in Jacques Haldy, Jean-Marc Rapp and Phidias Ferrari (eds); "Etudes de procédure et d'arbitrage en l'honneur de Jean-François Poudret", Faculté de droit de l'Université de Lausanne 1999, 387-402; Seraglini and Ortscheidt, *Droit de l'arbitrage interne et international,* cit., paras 664f.

31. French Code of Civil Procedure, article 1448.

32. Gaillard and Savage (eds.), "Fouchard Gaillard Goldman on International Commercial Arbitration", cit., paras 658 and 688; Seraglini and Ortscheidt, "Droit de l'arbitrage interne et international", cit., para 971.

33. See references in footnote above.

34. Luca Radicati di Brozolo, "Mandatory Rules and International Arbitration" (2012) 23 *American Rev. of Intl Arbitration*. 49; Seraglini and Ortscheidt, "Droit de l'arbitrage interne et international", cit., para 982. See also Cordero- Moss, "EU overriding mandatory rules", cit. and Cordero-Moss, "Mitsubishi", cit.

35. Cour d'appel de Paris, 1ère ch., 18.11.2004, *Rev arb*. 2005 751 (*Thalès Air Defence BV v.GIE Euromissile et al.*)

36. Gerechtshof Haag, 24.3.2005, NJF 2005/239, TvA 2006/24 (*Marketing Displays International Inc. v VR Van Raalte Reclame BV*).

37. For a Swiss decision following the minimalist approach see Tribunal fédéral, 4A_532/2014, 4A_534/2014, 29.1.2015.

38. See, in the areas of corruption and money laundering: Cour d'appel de Paris, 4.11.2014, nr. 13/10256; Cour d'appel de Paris, 25.11.2014, nr. 13/1333; Cour d'appel de Paris, 7.4.2015, nr. 14/00480; Cour d'appel de Paris, 14.4.2015, nr. 14/07043; Cour d'appel de Paris, 21.2.2017, nr. 15/01650; Cour d'appel de Paris, 16.1.2018, nr. 15/21703. *Contra*, see Cour d'appel de Paris, 20.1.2015, nr. 13/20318; Cour d'appel de Paris, 24.2.2015, nr. 13/23404. In the area of procedural fairness, see Cour d'appel de Paris, 8.11.2016, nr. 13/12002.

39. Born, "International Commercial Arbitration", cit., pp. 3312, 3647; Cordero-Moss, "International Commercial Contracts", cit., pp. 246ff.
40. As known, competition law has been deemed by the CJEU to be a matter of public policy in C-126/97 (Eco Swiss). For comments and further references, see Luca Radicati Di Brozolo, "Arbitration and Competition Law: The Position of the Courts and of Arbitrators", in *Arbitration International,* 2011, pp. 1–25. See also Cordero-Moss, "Inherent Powers and Competition Law", cit.
41. Radicati di Brozolo, "Mandatory Rules and International Arbitration", cit., pp. 63f.
42. Section 68 (2) (d).
43. Article 190 (2) (c). Other systems, such as the French system, do not permit setting aside an award that is *infra petita:* Judgment of 27 May 2010, *M. Cohen v Société Total Outre Mer SA*, Case No. 09/08191 (Paris Cour d'appel).
44. See G. Born, "International Commercial Arbitration", 2nd ed., 2014, p. 3294. For Singapore, see *CRW Joint Operation v PT Perusahaan Gas Negara (Persero) TBK [2011] SGCA 33; BLB and another v BLC and others [2013] S.G.H.C. 196, AKN and another v ALC* and others and other appeals [2015] SGCA 18. For Germany, see CLOUT case No. 375 [Bayerisches Oberstes Landesgericht, Germany, 4 Z Sch 23/99, 15 December 1999], also available on the Internet at http://www.dis-arb.de/de/47/datenbanken/rspr/bayoblg-az-4-z-sch-23-99-datum-1999-12-15-id16; Oberlandesgericht München, Germany, 34 Sch 12/09, 5 October 2009; Oberlandesgericht Frankfurt a.M., Germany, 26 Sch 01/03, 10 July 2003, available on the Internet at http://www.dis-arb.de/de/47/datenbanken/rspr/olg-frankfurt-amaz-26-sch-01-03-datum-2003-07-10-id226; Oberlandesgericht Frankfurt, Germany, 26 SchH 03/09, 27 August 2009. In that latter case, it was stated that the mere silence of the award on certain points raised by the defendant does not mean that the arbitral tribunal has not considered the argument, unless the specific circumstances of the case show the contrary, as for instance, when the argument is of crucial relevance for the legal outcome. Similarly, a court in Canada stated that the absence of reasons in the award does not mean that a party's right to be heard during the arbitration was violated: CLOUT case No. 30 [Ontario Court, General Division, Canada, *Robert E. Schreter v Gasmac Inc.*, 13 February 1992], [1992] O.J. No. 257. Not permitting to extend the rule of excess of power to an award *infra petita* see, for Hong Kong: *Brunswick Bowling & Billiards Corporation v Shanghai Zhonglu Industrial Co Ltd* [2009] HKCFI 94.
45. For references, see Giuditta Cordero-Moss, "The Arbitral Tribunal's Power in respect of the Parties' Pleadings as a Limit to Party Autonomy On Jura Novit Curia and Related Issues", in Franco Ferrari (ed.), *Limits to Party Autonomy in International Commercial Arbitration,* 289-330 (Juris, 2016), pp. 289-330, 305f.
46. See Cordero-Moss, *International Commercial Contracts,* cit, p. 90. See also Giuditta Cordero-Moss, *Boilerplate Clauses, International Commercial Contracts and the Applicable Law,* Cambridge University Press, 2011. More recently, Giuditta Cordero-Moss, "Detailed Contract Regulations and the UPICC: Parallels with National Law and Potential for Improvement—The Example of Norwegian Law", in *Essays in Honour of Michael Joachim Bonell* (UNIDROIT, 2016), pp. 1302-1317; Giuditta Cordero-Moss, "The importance of legal culture for contract construction: Norwegian Law, English Law and International Arbitration", *New York Dispute Resolution Lawyer (New York State Bar Association),* 2017, vol. 10, No 1, pp. 39-41.
47. Cordero-Moss, *International Commercial Contracts,* cit, p. 282.
48. Ivi, pp. 265-307; see also Giuditta Cordero-Moss, "Limitations on Party Autonomy in International Commercial Arbitration", *Collected Courses of The Hague Academy of International Law—Recueil des cours* 2015, Volume 372, pp. 133-326; for an extensive analysis of this question in 15 jurisdictions, Giuditta Cordero-Moss and Franco Ferrari (eds.), *Iura novit curia in arbitration,* Juris 2018, with General Report by Giuditta Cordero-Moss, "General Report on Jura Novit Arbiter", pp. 463-487. For further references, Cordero-Moss, "The Arbitral Tribunal's Power", cit., footnotes 37 to 39.
49. For a more extensive reasoning and references see Cordero-Moss, "EU Overriding Mandatory Provisions and the Law Applicable to the Merits", cit., p. 336f.
50. An example of such attempt, that so far has not proven particularly successful, can be found in a contract between Tiffany Company and The Swatch Group. The contract excluded from the power of the tribunal any possibility to change or add to the terms of the contract. The tribunal did not find this an obstacle to construing the contract so that a non-binding attachment was deemed to be a binding term. The award was set aside by the District Court of Amsterdam: case No C/13/567933/HA ZA 14-653, decision rendered on 5. March 2015. The Court of Appeal, however, confirmed the award: case No 200.170.351/01, decision rendered on 25. April 2017. For a more extensive description of the award and a comment on the District Court decision, see Cordero-Moss, "The Arbitral Tribunal's Power", cit., p. 319.

51. More extensively, Giuditta Cordero-Moss, "Conflict of laws as a basis to determine the arbitral tribunal's power sections", in Franco Ferrari and Stephan Kröll (eds.), *Conflict of laws in international arbitration, Juris* second edition forthcoming, sections VI, VII and VIII.
52. Cordero-Moss, "EU Overriding Mandatory Provisions", cit., pp. 339ff.
53. Cordero-Moss, "EU Overriding Mandatory Provisions", cit., pp. 341ff.
54. For example, the New York Convention contains choice of law rules regarding the law governing the capacity of the parties, the validity of the arbitration agreement, the arbitral procedure, arbitrability and public policy.
55. See Hague Conference on Private International Law, Principles on Choice of Law in International Commercial Contracts, March 19, 2015, art. 11(5).
56. Article 28(1).
57. Article 28(2).
58. According to the Model Law, the venue is the proper connecting factor for a series of important aspects, such as the validity of the arbitration agreement, the arbitral procedure, the tribunal's power to issue interim measures, the validity of the award and the applicable public policy—it does not seem unreasonable to consider it as a proper connecting factor also for the conflict rules. Some jurisdictions have formalised these considerations and instruct the tribunal to apply the private international law of the law of the venue, see the Norwegian Arbitration Act, 2004, § 31(2).
59. See the Swiss Private International Law Act, art. 187.
60. For example, Italian law.
61. See e.g. the French Code of Civil Procedure, art. 1511 and the 2019 Swedish Arbitration Act, article 27a.
62. See also Franco Ferrari and Stephan Kröll (eds.), "Conflict of laws in international arbitration", Juris 2010, second edition forthcoming.
63. See Hague Conference on Private International Law, Principles on Choice of Law in International Commercial Contracts, March 19, 2015, art. 11(5).
64. Luca Radicati di Brozolo, "Party autonomy and the rules governing the merits", in Franco Ferrari (ed.), "Limits to Party Autonomy in International Arbitration" , *Juris* 2016, pp. 331-362, 341f.
65. Extensively on the different bases that private international gives to select the applicable law, for example in respect of matters that are not covered by the parties' choice of law (such as preliminary questions of company law or security interests), in respect of matters where the parties' choice may be overridden (such as questions subject to competition law), see Cordero-Moss, "The arbitral tribunal's power", cit., pp. 308-314.
66. Radicati di Brozolo, "Mandatory Rules and International Arbitration", cit. p. 65.
67. For further comments see Cordero-Moss, "EU Overriding Mandatory Provisions", cit., pp. 345ff.
68. For a Canadian decision confirming this, see *Consolidated Contractors Group SAL v Abatovy Minerals SA* 2016 ONSC 7171.
69. See, for example, the Swiss Tribunal Fédéral decision in case 4A_254/2010. For further references and comments, see Andrea Bonomi and David Bochatay, "Iura novit arbiter in Swiss arbitration law", in Cordero-Moss and Ferrari (eds.), Iura novit curia in arbitration, cit., pp. 377-402; see also Cordero-Moss, "The arbitral tribunal's power", cit., pp. 318ff.
70. See, for example, the Swiss Tribunal Fédéral decision in case 4A_400/2008.
71. In some systems, such as in Norway and in Sweden, courts may independently revise the decision on costs: see the Norwegian Arbitration Act, § 39 (3), and article 41 of the Swedish Arbitration Act.
72. See, for example, Appendix VI to the 2017 ICC Rules of Arbitration, regulating expedited procedures (https://cdn.iccwbo.org/content/uploads/sites/3/2017/01/ICC-2017-Arbitration-and-2014-Mediation-Rules-english-version.pdf.pdf); the 2017 Stockholm Rules for Expedited Arbitrations (https://sccinstitute.com/media/178161/expedited_arbitration_rules_17_eng__web.pdf); Chapter VII of the 2017 Rules on Arbitration of the Oslo Chamber of Commerce Arbitration Institute, on Fast-track Arbitration (https://www.chamber.no/wp-content/uploads/2015/07/Rules-2017-Arbitration-English.pdf); the 2013 Rules of Simplified Arbitration by the Danish Institute of Arbitration (https://voldgiftsinstituttet.dk/wp-content/uploads/2015/04/rules-of-simplified-arbitration-2013.pdf); the 2013 Rules for Expedited Arbitration of the Finland Chamber of Commerce (https://arbitration.fi/arbitration/rules/rules-for-expedited-arbitration/)
73. Article 42 (1) of the 2017 Stockholm Rules for Expedited Arbitrations.
74. See article 4 of Appendix VI to the ICC Arbitration Rules.

75. See the ICC Notes to the parties and arbitral tribunals on the conduct of the arbitration, para 117.
76. See the Report of Working Group II (Dispute Settlement) on the work of its sixty-ninth session (New York, 4–8 February 2019), A/CN.9/969, https://undocs.org/en/A/CN.9/969, at item No 7.
77. Article 31 (2).
78. According to article 31 of the Swedish Arbitration Act, the only mandatory requirements for an award are signature, seat and date.
79. Article 51 of the Swedish Arbitration Act.
80. The Oslo Chamber of Commerce Rules of Arbitration, article 24 (4) have seen the difficulty and provide that the award shall state reasons, notwithstanding that the applicable Norwegian Arbitration Act permits the parties to agree to unreasoned awards: § 36 (6) of the 2004 Arbitration Act.
81. Such a waiver may be possible through the application of article VII of the New York Convention. This provision permits the courts to apply national law if the result is more favourable to the enforcement of an award than the provisions of the New York Convention. If the national law of the place of enforcement permits the parties to waive their right to resist enforcement, therefore, article VII of the New Yok Convention permits to apply this more favourable rule. I am not aware of any national law permitting such a waiver; see also Born, *International Commercial Arbitration,* cit., p. 3440f.
82. Sometimes, arbitral tribunals are expected to meet the same standards for stating reasons that are applicable to courts in the country where the tribunal has its seat. Norwegian courts, for example, have repeatedly applied to arbitral awards the provisions applicable to courts: LG-2010-175874 (Zachariasbryggen) and LE-2013-70296 (Hurum Energivinning). These decisions were rendered in connection with domestic arbitration, but under Norwegian arbitration law there is no difference between domestic and international arbitration.

Conclusion

by Mélida N. Hodgson

This dossier has taken us through a conceptual discussion of the issues surrounding reasoning in international arbitration to a discussion of practical aspects of reasoning that affect the practice of arbitration and its users. The authors ask should/if, and how, reasons be stated in various contexts. And a common thread through the chapters is the issue of legitimacy—reasoning, the lack or insufficiency thereof, impacts not only the specific recipients of an award, but can impact the legitimacy as a means of dispute resolution, particularly in the context of investment arbitration. But weighing against this pull for more may be the arbitral mantra of efficiency.

As a preliminary matter, reasons are stated as a justification for the arbitrators, the parties, the courts, and institutions. And sometimes there can be inconsistencies in what these constituents require (efficiency vs. detailed explanations). We also examine the standard of review to be applied to the duty to state reasons. In terms of substance, it is important for parties to know that all arguments have been considered, but we are reminded that neither the NY Convention or the UNCITRAL Model Law have as a ground for setting aside the failure to state reasons.

Further, civil law and common law arbitrators have similar concerns regarding the complexity of facts and of law, the importance of writing to refining reasoning, concern for the losing party, and, the legitimacy of the award. There is, however, some divergence—in concern about challenges to awards (civil law arbitrators care more) and legitimacy of the process rather than of the award itself (common law lawyers care more).

The story that a reasoned award tells is critical in the context of investment arbitration, simply because of the sheer numbers of people affected by an award.

And what do users of arbitration want? Not surprisingly, reasoning is a demonstration of the legitimacy of the award, evidence of the arbitrators' comprehension, and evidence that due process has been respected.

Although poor reasoning is not necessarily a reason for annulment, as elsewhere, there are certain minimum requirements (proof that facts, arguments, and evidence were considered) to satisfy a party's right to due process.

Of primary importance for users are valid and enforceable awards—that is, capable of withstanding the scrutiny of court control. But enforcement-proof reasoning also has to be convincing. The reasoning must be convincing to the parties, but also in order to withstand public policy scrutiny.

The call for "better" reasoning responds to calls for greater legitimacy in reasoning in both investment and commercial arbitration, from various audiences—some direct users, and some indirect users of arbitration. But there is a tension for arbitrators—the tension of efficiency, and what reviewing courts may actually require. Nonetheless, reasoning has such an impact, often beyond the principal litigants, that we can conclude from the contributions in this dossier that it may be time to outline certain basic standards for reasoning.

Contributors

About the Authors

Prof. Dr. Mohamed S. Abdel Wahab

Prof. Dr. Mohamed S. Abdel Wahab is the Chair of private international law and professor of international arbitration at Cairo University (Egypt); Founding Partner and Head of International Arbitration at Zulficar & Partners (Egypt); Vice President of the ICC International Court of Arbitration; Member of the Advisory Council of Africa Arbitration; Member of the CIMAC Court of Arbitration; Member of AAA-ICDR International Advisory Committee; Member of CIArb's Board of Trustees (MENA/Indian Subcontinent Regions); Member of the Advisory Committee of the CRCICA; Vice-Chair of the IBA Arab Regional Forum; Dean of the African Arbitration Academy; Member of the SIAC African Users Council Committee; Associate Fellow of the Centre of Private International Law at Aberdeen University (UK); Fellow of the Center for Technology and Dispute Resolution, University of Massachusetts (USA); Member of the ICODR's Governing Board; and Member of Arbitrator Intelligence's Board of Advisors. He is also an International Expert Member of the Permanent Forum of China Construction Law; Member of the Editorial Board of the CIArb's *Arbitration Journal*; Member of the Editorial Advisory Board of the *Journal of Enforcement of Arbitration Awards*; Member of the Editorial Board of the *IBA Journal of Construction Law International*; and Co-Editor of *Online Dispute Resolution: Theory and Practice* (2012), which received the CPR Award for the Best Published Dispute Resolution Work (2013). He served as "Sole", "Presiding" and "Party Appointed" Arbitrator, "Counsel" and "Legal Expert" in more than 190 cases. He appeared in cases under the auspices of the AAA, AAA-BCDR, CRCICA, DIAC, DIFC-LCIA, ICC, ICSID, LCIA, LMAA, SCC, SIAC, as well as ad hoc UNCITRAL proceedings. recognized as a world-leading arbitrator and arbitration practitioner on international investment and international commercial arbitration, Arab and African Laws and Islamic Shari'a. He acted as "counsel" and served as "arbitrator" in proceedings governed by Bahraini, Egyptian, English, French, Iraqi, Jordanian, Kuwaiti, Libyan, Moroccan, New York, Omani, Pakistani, Qatari, Saudi, Spanish, Swiss, Syrian, Italian and United Arab Emirates law(s), as well as the general principles of law.

In 2018, Prof. Dr. Abdel Wahab received the Swiss Arbitration Association's International Arbitration Global Advocacy Prize. He features in AFRICA's 100 list of African arbitration practitioners by I-ARB (Africa) and was selected by Africa Arbitration as the African Personality of the Month (June 2018) and by the LACIAC (Lagos Chamber of Commerce International Arbitration Centre) as the Arbitration Personality in May 2019. Nominated for the GAR Award for the Best Arbitration Lecture in 2013, 2014and 2018. He is appointed as the Dean of African Arbitration Academy, London (June 2019) and was the CIArb's Diploma Director for the International Arbitration Diploma, Oxford (September 2019).

In June 2019, Prof. Dr. Abdel Wahab received the AYA Hall of Fame Award in London for the African Arbitrator of 2019. He features in *Who's Who Legal: Arbitration*; *GAR Global Guide for Future Leaders in International Arbitration* (2017-2018); and *Who's Who Legal Thought Leaders: International Arbitration* (2017-2018). *Who's Who Legal* (2017-2018) says: Mohamed Abdel Wahab is "one of the best practitioners in the world today", and in 2019 *Who's Who Legal* says: Mohamed Abdel Wahab is "a leader in the space" who is "at the top of the market". He is described as "a star" who offers "practical advice and a tireless approach".

Giuditta Cordero-Moss Dr. juris (Oslo), PhD (Moscow), is professor at the University of Oslo.

Her fields of expertise are primarily International Commercial Law, International Commercial Arbitration, Private International Law, Comparative Contract Law and Norwegian Law of Obligations.

An originally Italian lawyer, before joining the Oslo University she practiced the law of international contracts for nearly 20 years in the areas of financing, as well as commercial and industrial cooperation.

She has published numerous books and articles in Norway and internationally. A list of publications may be found here: http://folk.uio.no/giudittm/GCM_List%20of%20Publications.htm She is often invited by universities and organisations, including the Hague Academy of International Law—where she held a series of lectures on Party Autonomy in International Commercial Arbitration (2014).

Since 2002 she acts as an arbitrator in her areas of expertise in a variety of arbitral institutions: Central Chamber of Commerce of Finland, Danish Institute of Arbitration, International Arbitration Court at the Russian Chamber of Commerce and Industry, International Chamber of Commerce, Oslo Chamber of Commerce, Stockholm Chamber of Commerce, Vienna International Arbitral Centre, as well as in ad hoc proceedings.

Since 2017 she is President of the Administrative Tribunal, European Bank for Reconstruction and Development, where she has been a judge since 2007.

She holds positions in numerous organisations, among others: Member of the Curatorium of the Hague Academy of International Law (since 2019), Alternate Member of the International Court of Arbitration, International Chamber of Commerce (since 2018), member of the Norwegian Governmental Tariff Board (since 2015), Vice Chairman of the Board of the Financial Supervisory Authority of Norway (since 2014), delegate for Norway at the UNCITRAL Working Group on Arbitration (since 2007).

Teresa B. Giovannini is a founding partner of LALIVE (since 1994) and specialises in international arbitration. She has acted as counsel or arbitrator in more than 200 international arbitrations, including setting aside proceedings before the Swiss Supreme Court, either ad hoc (e.g. under UNCITRAL Rules) or administered by institutions such as the AAA/ICDR, CAM, ICC, ICSID, LCIA and SCC.

Ms Giovannini is the Swiss member of the ICC Court of Arbitration and of the Council of the ICC Institute of World Business Law. She was a member and vice-president of the LCIA Court (2006–2011) and a member of the Arbitral Council of the Milan Chamber of Arbitration (CAM) (1997–2005), the Board of Directors of the American Arbitration Association (AAA), the Executive Council of the CPR European Advisory Board (2013–2019) and Panel of Distinguished Neutrals, the Club of Arbitrators of the Milan Chamber of National and International Arbitration, the Advisory Board of the Institute for Transnational Arbitration (ITA).

Teresa Giovannini is a frequent speaker and lecturer on international arbitration (including at Columbia Law School; the Fordham University School of Law and Harvard Law School; the International Chamber of Commerce; the Chartered Institute of Arbitrators (Clarb); the University of Oxford, Queen's College; IBA; ITA; etc.) She has been ranked for many years as a leading arbitration practitioner by Chambers Europe and Chambers Global for Dispute resolution—Arbitrators for Switzerland, and as a Thought Leader in Arbitration by Who's Who Legal. She was listed among the Best Prepared/Most Responsive Arbitrators by Global Arbitration Review (GAR).

Anja Ipp is legal counsel at the Arbitration Institute of the Stockholm Chamber of Commerce (SCC) since 2015. In that capacity, she has overseen the administration of several hundred arbitrations, and regularly contributes to the development of SCC procedures and policies. She is a board member of Young Arbitrators Sweden (YAS) and the Swedish Women in Arbitration Network (SWAN) and serves on the editorial committee of the Stockholm Arbitration Yearbook. Before joining the SCC in 2015, Anja was an associate in the global disputes practice of Jones Day in New York. She holds a JD from Columbia University, an LLM from the University of Amsterdam, and a BA from Lund University.

Charles Jarrosson is Professor at the University of Paris II Panthéon-Assas where he teaches Arbitration and ADR and manages the post-graduate Master Litigation, Arbitration & ADR. He is also visiting professor in different foreign universities, especially in Lebanon. He is editor in chief of the Revue de l'arbitrage, and vice-president of the French National Committee of the ICC.

He has acted in more than one hundred and forty arbitration procedures, as arbitrator (Chairman of the arbitral tribunal, sole arbitrator, party-appointed arbitrator) in domestic or international arbitrations, ad hoc or ICC, or ICSID, or under the aegis of other institutions. The arbitrations have been conducted in French, English or Italian.

Numerous experiences of counsel in arbitrations. Experiences of consultant for arbitration institutions. Ex-Member of the Court of Arbitration of the Camera arbitrale nazionale e internazionale di Milano (2003–2008). He has acted in mediations, and in other ADRs.

He is a member of the Board of the Comité français de l'arbitrage; Scientific coordinator of Ispramed. He is also a member of International Arbitration Institute (IAI); Association française d'arbitrage (AFA); Association suisse d'arbitrage (ASA); Comité français de droit international privé.

Publications: *La notion d'arbitrage* LGDJ ed., 1987 as well as numerous papers and caselaw commentaries in different law reviews.

Luca G. Radicati di Brozolo

Partner, ARBLIT—Radicati di Brozolo Sabatini Benedettelli Torsello, Italy; Professor, Catholic University of Milan

Professor Luca G. Radicati di Brozolo is an internationally recognized academic and practitioner now predominantly active in international commercial and investor-State arbitration.

After practicing in many different areas of law for many years as a partner in two of the major Italian firms, in 2013 he founded the arbitration and litigation boutique ArbLit—Radicati di Brozolo Sabatini Benedettelli Torsello (www.arblit.com). He has a very active practice as presiding, party-appointed and sole arbitrator, counsel and expert in arbitral proceedings under the main arbitration rules and in many different seats and involving a broad array of issues and applicable laws. He has significant experience in investor-State arbitration and appears in court litigation as counsel and expert witness in arbitration-related cases and cases raising issues of international and competition law.

Luca is a door tenant at Fountain Court Chambers in London, listed on the ICSID Panel of Arbitrators appointed by Italy, Vice-President of the Court of the London Court of International Arbitration and a member of numerous scientific and professional organizations. He is a former member of the ICC International Court of Arbitration and former Vice-Chair of the IBA Arbitration Committee, a member and former rapporteur of the Committee on International Commercial Arbitration of the International Law Association and a former co-chair of the Joint Working Group of the Competition and Arbitration Committees of the ICC Arbitration Commission on Antitrust Follow-on Actions.

As an academic, his scholarship has been devoted primarily to private international law, the law of arbitration, public international law, European Union law and antitrust law. He held the chair of Private International Law at the Catholic University of Milan, where he also taught Law of International Arbitration until October 2019. He is the author of five books and nearly 200 scholarly articles in major law reviews and publications and is a co-editor of the leading Italian commentary of the law of arbitration, now in its second edition, and a frequent speaker at academic and professional conferences and event. He has held positions in various foreign universities, and in 2003 held a special course on international arbitration in the private international law session at the Hague Academy of International Law where in 2018 he held the General Course in Private International Law on "The Legal Framework of International Commercial Relations".

S.I. Strong specializes in international dispute resolution and comparative law, with a particular emphasis on international commercial arbitration and large-scale (class and collective) suits. Dr. Strong is currently an Associate Professor of Law at the University of Sydney and has taught at the Universities of Cambridge and Oxford in the United Kingdom as well as Georgetown Law Center and the University of Missouri in the United States. Dr. Strong has published over 100 award-winning books and articles in Europe, Asia and the Americas and is an experienced practitioner, having acted as Counsel at Baker & McKenzie after working as a dual-qualified lawyer (US attorney and English solicitor) in the New York and London offices of Weil, Gotshal & Manges. Dr. Strong, who holds a PhD in law from the University of Cambridge, a DPhil from the University of Oxford, a JD from Duke University, an MPW from the University of Southern California and a BA from the University of California, Davis, sits as an arbitrator on a variety of international commercial and trust-related matters.

Contributors

About the Editors

Antonio Crivellaro Founder of Arbitration Practice at BonelliErede, Italy; Council Member, ICC Institute of World Business Law

Antonio Crivellaro is a former Professor of International Law and International Trade Law. He is a former Partner and currently Emeritus Partner at Bonelli Erede, Milan office, where he founded the International Arbitration Group. He has extensive experience (more than 250 cases in a period of 40 years) in international—commercial and investment—arbitration as either counsel, or arbitrator, or chairman in several arbitral institutions (ICC; ICSID; LCIA; SCA; Cairo Centre; Bangkok Centre; Milan Chamber, Dubai-DIAC Arbitration Centre) and ad hoc proceedings. Recommended as "Leading" arbitrator in international cases relating to investment, construction, energy, industrial supply by Chambers and other Dispute Resolution sources worldwide.

His area of expertise includes disputes arising from contracts for gas and oil projects, works and concessions, industrial plants, supplies and sales, financing and banking operations, telecommunications and post-closing M&A disputes. He further specializes in international investment law and investor-to-State arbitrations. Appointed by Italy as Member of the ICSID List of Arbitrators. Member and Italian correspondent of the *Institut de l'Arbitrage International (IAI) Paris*.

He is a Council Member of the ICC Institute of World Business Law and author of a number of publications in international contracts and arbitration law. He is Editor in Chief of *Diritto del Commercio Internazionale—The Law of International Trade*.

Mélida N. Hodgson Partner Jenner & Block, USA

Mélida N. Hodgson focuses her practice on investor-state and commercial arbitration, counseling governments and state-owned entities with respect to international investment protection obligations, business disputes, as well as advising on World Trade Organization dispute resolution and policy issues. She has extensive experience in leading infrastructure, energy, and contract disputes before the International Centre for Settlement of Investment Disputes (ICSID), United Nations Commission on International Trade Law (UNCITRAL) tribunals, International Chamber of Commerce (ICC) and WTO panels. She is also an arbitrator.

Ms Hodgson is a member of the ICC Commission on Arbitration and ADR, the ICC Institute of World Business Law Council, the Executive Council of the American Society of International Law, and the Council of the American Arbitration Association.

Ms Hodgson has been recognized by Latinvex as one of the top 50 female practitioners and top 100 lawyers whose practice focuses on Latin America, and she also has been ranked by *Chambers Global*, *USA*, and *Latin America* editions, and noted in *Legal 500 Latin America* and *Who's Who Arbitration*.

She is fluent in Spanish and conducts proceedings in English and Spanish. Ms Hodgson is a founding member of the Washington Women in International Arbitration.

Cases

Collection of ICC Arbitral Awards 2008-2011

ICC Pub. No. 748EF, €265

his collection of ICC Arbitral Awards is a vital reference for cholars and practitioners of international arbitration alike. This dition supplements five previous and successful volumes. ogether, they cover nearly 40 years of work of the ICC Court of rbitration. In addition to providing a wealth of information in a ighly accessible manner, it includes case notes end expert ommentaries on the awards.

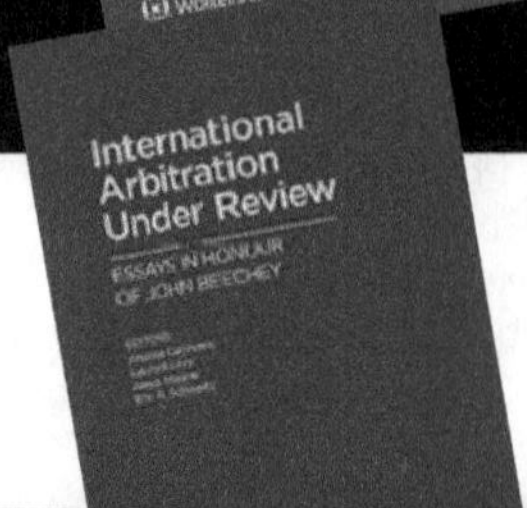

International Arbitration Under Review

Essays in honour of John Beechey

Edited by Andrea Carlevaris, Laurent Lévy, Alexis Mourre and Eric A. Schwartz
ICC Pub. No. 772E, €135

This collection of 34 articles provides informed commentary by leading arbitration specialists on some of today's most pressing subjects, including procedural efficiency, arbitrator independence and investor-state dispute settlement (ISDS). The book also contains articles on arbitral appeal procedures, responsibilities of institutions, dissenting opinions, remission of awards, use of arbitration in disputes arising from mass disasters, and party representation by foreign lawyers.

Summaries of UAE Courts' Decisions on Arbitration 2012-2016

Including DIFC Courts decisions—Second Edition

Edited by Hassan Arab, Lara Hammoud and Graham Lovett
ICC Pub. No. 789E, €68

his second edition comprises 43 carefully selected recent dgments (2012-2016) from the Federal Supreme Court, the Abu habi Court of Cassation, Dubai Court of Cassation and the DIFC ourts.

Summaries of UAE Court's Decisions on Arbitration

ICC Pub. No. 746E, €61.20 (eBook)

his collection of arbitration case summaries and judgements rovides insight into how arbitration works and how it is treated y the judiciary in the United Arab Emirates (UAE). A helpful tool r lawyers, arbitrators and other professionals involved in UAE lated arbitration proceedings.

Dispute Resolution and Climate Change

Edited by Wendy Miles
ICC Pub. No. 778E, €49 (eBook)

This ePublication brings together articles from 18 international dispute resolution and/or climate change specialists who explore ways in which climate change issues may be factored into existing processes and systems of international dispute resolution, in particular international arbitration.

Hardship and Force Majeure in International Commercial Contracts | Dealing with unforeseen events in a changing world

Dossier XVII of the ICC Institute of World Business Law

Edited by Fabio Bortolotti and Dorothy Ufot
ICC Pub. No. 796 E, €75

Parties need to be able to analyse the nature and characteristics of force majeure and hardship and look for contractual clauses which can regulate these issues in conformity with their needs. Written by international practitioners, this dossier explores the evolution of the rules on hardship, the ICC Clause on Hardship and the perspectives of contract adaptation by arbitrators.

The section on Force Majeure includes an overview of recent arbitral case law, analysis of the ICC 2003 Force Majeure Clause and an update on its revision.

Expedited Procedures in International Arbitration

Dossier XVI of the ICC Institute of World Business Law

Edited by Laurent Lévy and Michael Polkinghorne
ICC Pub. No. 793E, €75

The amended ICC Rules of Arbitration entered into force on 1 March 2017. They include an ICC expedited procedure automatically applicable to cases with an amount in dispute below USD 2 million unless expressly excluded by the parties. This Dossier explores some of the ways and means to conduct proceedings in a reasonable time without jeopardising due process.

Dispute Prevention and Settlement through Expert Determination and Dispute Boards

Dossier XV of the ICC Institute of World Business Law

Edited by Filip De Ly, Paul-A. Gélinas
ICC Pub. No. 792E, €75

Thirteen international experts share their knowledge and their experience on the impact of applicable law, contract law issues, procedural issues and the relationship between Expert Determination or Dispute Boards on the one hand and litigation and arbitration on the other.

Class and Group Actions in Arbitration

Dossier XIV of the ICC Institute of World Business Law

Edited by Bernard Hanotiau and Eric Schwartz
ICC Pub. No. 771E, €75

Is there a place for such proceedings within the framework of the arbitration process? Class action procedures, as developed in the United States court system and more recently in Canada, are almost nonexistent in Europe. The book highlights the lessons learned from cases in the US and in Europe.

About the International Chamber of Commerce (ICC)

The International Chamber of Commerce (ICC) is the institutional representative of more than 45 million companies in over 100 countries. ICC's core mission is to make business work for everyone, every day, everywhere. Through a unique mix of advocacy, solutions and standard setting, we promote international trade, responsible business conduct and a global approach to regulation, in addition to providing market-leading dispute resolution services. Our members include many of the world's leading companies, SMEs, business associations and local chambers of commerce.

www.iccwbo.org

Follow us on Twitter: @iccwbo

www.ingramcontent.com/pod-product-compliance
Lightning Source LLC
Chambersburg PA
CBHW071350230926
51846CB00002B/491
9789403529035